D1500128

Violence and Social Change

VIOLENCE AND SOCIAL CHANGE

Henry Bienen

A Review of Current Literature

*Anything can grow out of
the barrel of a gun.*
—Mao Tse-tung

Published for
The Adlai Stevenson Institute of
International Affairs

The University of Chicago Press
Chicago and London

ISBN: 0-226-04760-1 (clothbound); 0-226-04762-8—(paperbou

Library of Congress Catalog Card Number: 68-56012

The University of Chicago Press, Chicago 60637
The University of Chicago Press, Ltd., London

In Memory of My Mother
PEARL WITTY BIENEN
1910-1967

CONTENTS

FOREWORD

In the summer of 1967 the Adlai Stevenson Institute of
International Affairs established a study group on violent
politics and modernization. The purpose was to review and
hopefully to deepen the present state of knowledge about
the relationship between violence and rapid social change.
As organized by Professor Manfred Halpern of Princeton
University, a Fellow of the Institute, and Wayne Fredericks,
former Deputy Assistant Secretary of State for African Affairs and now of the Ford Foundation, a group of distinguished social scientists met each month to consider papers
on various aspects of modernization and violence.

This book is based on the first working paper prepared
for the seminar by Professor Henry Bienen of Princeton
University. Realizing that we were moving into a difficult,
emotion-fraught, and largely uncharted field, the group
sought in Professor Bienen's study a dispassionate descrip-
tion and assessment of contemporary writings on various
aspects of our problem. In this it was not disappointed.
Indeed, so valuable did we find the paper that we asked
Professor Bienen to expand and revise it for publication.

On the foundation created by Professor Bienen's work,
a series of papers presented to the study group deal with
various aspects of the problem of violence and social change.
The group considered works by Manfred Halpern on the

nature of modernization, William Kornhauser of the University of California (Berkeley) on order and change in the universities, John T. McAlister of Princeton on the revolutionary origins of the Vietnamese war, Charles V. Hamilton of Roosevelt University on characteristics of leadership in the American black community, and Morris Janowitz of the University of Chicago on control of escalated riots. Other participants shared with the group their work in progress on large-scale revolutionary movements, revolts, disorders in American cities, and unrest in university communities. A sustained effort was made to emphasize the comparative nature of aspects of violence and social change not only in a regional sense, between the United States and other areas, but also in different kinds of social institutions.

Professor Bienen's book sketches many of the problems still only partially understood after the first year's effort. With great perception it distinguishes between lines of inquiry which seem fruitful and those which do not, and analyzes some of the areas which will require major attention if scholars are to make sense of the phenomena of violent politics. Unfortunately, as Professor Bienen points out, there is little systematic work available which even defines what is meant by "change," and we are very far from understanding the major examples of modern violent politics: ghetto violence, guerrilla warfare, revolution, and totalitarianism. Without restricting himself to a narrow definition of his subject, Professor Bienen deals with writers from Machiavelli to Debray to elucidate the dimensions of previous discussions on violence and change. He indicates areas of disagreements in the literature as a first step toward resolution and identifies those dark areas which previous scholars have failed to illuminate.

This study and other aspects of the Stevenson Institute seminar on violent politics were made possible by a generous donation from the Marshall Field Foundation of New York in memory of Eleanor Roosevelt.

The members of the working group included, in addition to those mentioned above, Professors Eqbal Ahmad of Cornell University, Leonard Binder of the University of Chicago, J. David Greenstone of the University of Chicago, Edward T. Gude of Dartmouth College, Mohammed Guessous of Princeton University, Samuel Huntington of Harvard University, Aristide Zolberg of the University of Chicago, Edward Shils of the University of Chicago, M. Crawford Young of the University of Wisconsin, and Marvin Zonis of the University of Chicago. Additionally, the following Fellows of the Adlai Stevenson Institute participated: Frederick S. Arkhurst, Brian Beun, Abdelhafeez El-Rufaie, Abdul Kayeum, Kanta Khipple, Richard Pfeffer, A. David Rossin, Richard Rubenstein, and M. Stephen Kaplan, Research Associate.

In the second year of our work on violent politics, the Institute staff and Fellows are attempting to assemble from these and other materials a curriculum aimed at elucidating the complex interrelationships of violence and change for those who have taken major responsibility in political decision-making at local, state, federal, and international levels. Surely there is no more dangerous or demanding issue before us in the last third of the twentieth century. Professor Bienen has here performed a valuable service in analyzing the ways in which scholars and practitioners have dealt with this crucial subject.

William R. Polk
Director

PREFACE

This essay is a revision of a working paper I presented to the study group on violent politics and modernization of the Adlai Stevenson Institute of International Affairs; it remains a working paper. Since the period October, 1967, to February, 1968, when some revisions were made, a number of interesting articles and books dealing with violence and social change have been published. But I did not try to keep abreast of new works in these pages any more than I tried to be inclusive in my treatment of earlier published material. The revisions made between October and February take account of criticisms voiced at the presentation of the first draft and of those made by other readers since then. I did extend the number of works that were concerned with violence in American cities, largely because to some extent I had neglected treatments which argue that violence in the ghetto is a response to violence used by outsiders in the ghetto.

I deeply appreciate the comments made on the first draft of this essay by the study group on violent politics of the Adlai Stevenson Institute of International Affairs. I used those comments as I saw fit in making revisions. To Professor Manfred Halpern I owe a special debt for his encouragement of and enthusiasm for this effort. I am particularly grateful for his thoughtful criticisms and those of Professors Marion Levy, Jr., and Edward Schneier, of Princeton University. Sometimes

I took their advice, but they, of course, bear no responsibility for the selective use I made of their views. The Center of International Studies at Princeton University supported this work by providing release time and typing assistance. I am grateful to Klaus Knorr, director of the Center, for his support of my efforts.

Permission to reprint the last stanza from "The Rose Tree," by William Butler Yeats, from *The Collected Poems of W. B. Yeats,* has been granted by Macmillan Co. (New York), and by M. B. Yeats and Macmillan & Co. Ltd. (London). Reprinted with permission of The Macmillan Company from *The Collected Poems of William Butler Yeats,* copyright 1924 by The Macmillan Company; renewed 1952 by Bertha Georgie Yeats.

INTRODUCTION

When I was asked to present the first paper to the Adlai Stevenson Institute's study group on violent politics and modernization, I was charged with reviewing present scholarly knowledge and implicit policy assumptions about violence so that we might discuss the relationship of that knowledge to the subject of modernization. Thus the primary question I had in mind when starting this undertaking was: How do various works on violence clarify thinking about change and, in particular, thinking about what is called modernization? That I began with literatures ostensibly devoted to violence does not mean that I think one necessarily should start with analyzing violence in order to come to grips with problems of social change, although violence as a prism for seeing change has not been well exploited. Furthermore, there is an advantage for a study group devoted to getting close to problems of social change in starting with works on violence, for many of these strain after the problems, although they do not usually clarify issues. If we had started with modernization, we should have found less on violence.

It was pointed out in the discussions of the first draft of this essay that violence subsumes so much that we cannot formulate good theories which account for it. It was also pointed out, in reply to my pessimistic conclusions concerning what we know, that there has been a useful and extensive literature on typologies of violence. There is an answer to both points. We know less about the causes and consequences of violence, and especially the consequences, than we do about the scope, intensity, and duration of violence under certain circumstances. This reflects our relative ability to distinguish between aspects of violence as compared with our ability to link violence and change. Some of the most useful writings I encountered were concerned above all to distinguish typologies of violence not merely in terms of frequency, duration, and scope but also in terms of kinds of systems and kinds of change. But most typologies of violence do not do this; once this is done, violence does not subsume so much, because we can root violence in defined contexts. The issue is not creating typologies of violence per se but clarifying problems of social change.

What follows is my examination of where we are. I have not drawn my own position on violence and modernization, although I do not state others' arguments only. I try to indicate promising paths and what has been neglected, and to criticize certain endeavors and applaud others.

The aim of the study group on violent politics and modernization was to analyze rapid, fundamental, worldwide, and often violent change. Every modifier of change except "worldwide" creates difficulties for me because I admit to being uncertain about what constitutes rapid, fundamental change; thus obviously I am in some difficulty over what change means, lacking criteria for specifying degrees of change. It is one thing to be able to differentiate between an avalanche and a snowball and another to be able to distinguish in the realm of social change without committing a host of fallacies—of misplaced dichotomies, of reification, of circular concepts. (Levy [1967] has recently discussed these fallacies.)[1] This must be said straight off, because (1) a concern for violence and change leads one to the literature on revolution where these fallacies among others are rife, and (2) discussions of modernization involving definitions of the category and processes to be analyzed again involve one in a concern for end-states to be arrived at—or more usefully, but not without problems also, in concern for kinds and rates of change or transformation. Because there has been a proliferation of definitions of modernization (Westernization, rationalization and bureaucratization, systematic and persistent transformation, economic development, social mobilization, institutionalized politics, democracy, etc.), it seemed wisest for me to adopt Alice's position in Wonderland. How do I know what I want to read until I read it? That is, since there has been no established paradigm of modernization, I could not be reading about violence with the aim of getting new insights for an established body of knowledge or a framework within which studies of violence could themselves be set. Rather, I was reading on violence to see whether bodies of literature got us any further in thinking about what has been variously called modernization.

Happily, there were fewer problems with the concept of violence, although there are important conceptual and definitional questions to raise about violence. Men have been slaying each other since Cain and Abel, and we have a pretty good idea of what we mean by violence, at least insofar as

---

1. Year of publication is cited only if more than one work by the author is mentioned in this volume. Page numbers, when listed, refer to the writings under discussion. See Bibliography for full details of publication.

it is synonymous with physical aggression which we can measure for intensity, frequency, and duration. Nonetheless, the word violence carries overtones of "violating," and we often use violence to refer to illegitimate force (Leys, p. 17). When the police uphold law and order we sometimes refer to their use of force, and we sometimes make reference to police oppression if the legitimacy of their actions is called in question. When force is considered to be legitimate, many people do not equate it with violence. Thus violence is distinguished from coercion. The above is meant to suggest that there are problems entailed by the use of the word violence. These problems have led Wolin to define violence as force exercised with unnecessary intensity, unpredictability, or unusual destructiveness. And they led Johnson (1967, pp. 7-10) to define violence as either behavior which is impossible for others to orient themselves to or as behavior which is deliberately intended to prevent orientation and the development of stable expectations with regard to it. (I discuss some difficulties which flow from these definitions in chapter 3, on revolution.)

Another difficulty arises when we consider that violence in the sense of violating or forcing often does not involve physical constraints at all; there is violence against the body, but there is also a sense of doing violence to someone's psyche or livelihood. In both cases extremes of action are being noted, e.g., psychological warfare. There is also the interesting question of the political relevance of violence. Judgments here have been usually ex post facto. After large-scale domestic warfare, commentators look again at criminal acts to see if a rise in salience of crime precedes a rise in violence where overtly political demands are made and political consequences follow. At present, an indicator for anticipation of internal warfare is thought of as some deviance in the pattern of crime or violence against individuals. (We do not seem to be sure if rising or decreasing rates of crime in the ghetto indicate coming civil strife, the latter perhaps indicating a shift of aggression against self, or someone like oneself, to a different social target.) Most questions *about* the political relevance of violence seemed to be raised in works on criminology or deviant personalities rather than in works on internal war or revolution, where political relevance is taken for granted.

My own approach to the problem of definitions and of political relevance was largely to ignore them by selecting out of the literature on violence certain headings under which subliteratures could be grouped—those where political relevance was already assumed. The subheadings I made were a matter of convenience in organizing work rather than units which have analytical bite to them. Thus I looked at writing on (1) ghetto violence (but not on racial violence per se); (2) internal war, which included guerrilla warfare, and counterinsurgency, civil war, coups, and riots; (3) revolution, which embraces both categories (1) and (2) *if* one assumes that certain propensities of violence arise from or give rise to kinds of social change; (4) works devoted to the structure of violence, typologies of violence, and the romance of violence; (5) totalitarianism. It is clear that these are overlapping and untidy categories, and category (4) has no subhead in this paper.

At least two important bodies of literature are left out. One deals with the linkages between international violence and domestic social change, including foreign sponsorship of domestic violence. Its absence reflects constraints on time and energy only. The other focuses on instruments of violence, the military and police. The role of the military as a modernizing force has occupied the broad efforts of the Inter-University Seminar on Armed Forces and Society, and I have commented on it elsewhere *(The Military Intervenes: Case Studies in Political Change)*.

I made no attempt to be all-inclusive in searching out books and articles. Nor did I start from ancient wisdom and work myself up chronologically. Rather, I tried to find theme which were sounded again and again, or rarely, largely in contemporary commentaries, and to juxtapose them; to point out contradictions as well as complementarities. Above all, I tried to indicate where the literature seems to give definite, tentative, or no answers. The striking lacunas in the literature raise questions about the study of violence.

One may value a decline in violence as a goal of politics. But this value should not restrain analysts and policymakers from attempting to understand violence. To treat violence and far-reaching social change as pathological phenomena does hinder analysis. Yet much of the literature, including works by those who romanticize violence, does treat violence as a phenomenon outside of a "normal" social process.

This is especially true for much of American social science work on violence and has particular force when we consider studies of violence in America. In this review of the "state of the art," it is apparent to me that chapter 1, on ghetto violence, is less satisfactory than the other chapters. In part, this may stem from my relative lack of familiarity with the relevant material. But there is a more serious factor at work. Compared with the literature on revolution, guerrilla warfare, and totalitarianism, there is much less relevant material on domestic violence. The study of violence in America has been less advanced even than the study of guerrilla warfare. Why should social science study of violence in general and analysis of domestic violence in particular be so inadequate?

Surely, as Harry Eckstein (1964, p. 3) pointed out, there is nothing in the world of political events that can account for the relative neglect of violence in social science analyses in the past. Eckstein offered the view that in studies of what he called internal war the subject has not been processed theoretically, and thus social scientists, confronting the welter of empirical materials, have not been able to bridge the gulf between theoretical schema and empirical work (pp. 5-6). Moreover, Eckstein argued, the difficulties in applying rigorous analysis, making use of quantitative techniques and controlled experiments, have led social scientists to shy away from internal war as a field relatively unsuited to contemporary social science research. All this may be true, but it does not seem to me to go far enough.

Perhaps there is something in the theoretical and methodological perspectives of social scientists (including historians) which prevents them from exploring group violence and its consequences for social change beyond their limiting concern for precision and analytical rigor. One might want to ask: What kinds of interests and prejudices—personal, professional, national—have shaped the study of violent politics? On the personal and professional levels, certain biases and interests may be shared by social scientists across national boundaries. For one thing, violence may be perceived as something that must be experienced directly if one is to write and think adequately about it. Since the consequences of violence may be presumed to be great, at least for an individual or social group, social scientists dealing with abstract systems may have stepped away from its study. Furthermore, precisely because violence has been presumed to be destabilizing, leading to anarchy and to incoherence, social scientists may have thought that once this was pointed out there was little more to say. But a prior question arises: Why have such attitudes been prevalent, if indeed they have? Here I would confine a few remarks to American investigators of violence and social change.

The techniques of contemporary social science and the perspectives of political scientists, sociologists, and historians must be understood as being formed in a given society or set of subsocieties. Perhaps what has been considered a legitimate field of study depends, in part, on what is considered a legitimate form of social action. If forms of social action are thought of as taking place along a possible continuum of violence—from interest-group demands which involve pressure to acts of physical force—it is clear that different groups in society as well as societal norms as a whole define as legitimate some actions under various conditions. American society, which has raised the process of bargaining over interests that can be accommodated to a goal of the system, has also been the home of numerous political studies of this process. On the other hand, the lack of studies on violence may be understood in terms of the view many hold of violence as an illegitimate means of settling disputes. It is striking that in the last year or so there has been a marked increase in the number of new studies dealing with violence, symposia on violence, concern in the press with violence; this may

be related not only to the increase in violence and its saliency but perhaps also to a different view of the legitimacy
of the use of violence by black persons. As attitudes get abandoned, traditional techniques of inquiry may change too.

We are in an area where a great deal of new work is called
for. Questions about the whys of violence remain very open.
From the literature on violent politics we know about the
components or factors leading to violence, but we do not
know about combinations and sequences. We so far still know
only in an imprecise way what we mean by change and what
kinds of change we ought to be fostering by conscious policy
decisions. Above all, the relationship between violence and
modernization remains one that in the literature cuts many
ways at once. No case studies seem persuasive in establishing
the relationships. No general propositions seem able to en-
compass all the "on the one hand this and on the other thats."
In particular, I was struck by the fact that it is predominantly
in studies of totalitarianism that violence as a tool of inno-
vating elites is examined; elsewhere, violence for innovation
is relatively neglected. Similarly, organization-building through
violent politics and the use of organizations for violence have
been treated almost exclusively in terms of secret-police studies. Yet in the works of famous insurgents, time and again
the theme is sounded that, through violence, organizations
can be constructed and modernization achieved. Theories of
political development which stress institutionalization must
confront the possibility that political institutions will be
used for violence and must specify the conditions under
which this is possible and likely, and where violence may
be a substitute for change.

There is now in vogue a literature on rebirth through

commitment to violence. This literature has a rather ancient pedigree, although in the past those who argued for rebirth through violence often referred to a rebirth after death which would come from participation in some holy war. Many chiliastic movements made this claim, one which social science is hard put to test. But now, Sorel's assertion that a class can be resurrected through violence, or Fanon's argument that individuals and peoples can become whole again by participating in violent politics, or the Gandhian claim for the therapeutic results of nonviolence can be judged because the claims are for the here and now. Is it true that group and individual transformations take place through violence? Is violence primarily engaged in to change oneself rather than a social condition, or engaged in with almost no instrumental concerns at all, but rather for the immediate gratifications derived from its exercise? Societies may assign goals to group which are undertaking violent politics, perhaps because these are the goals the larger society can deal with, when the motivations for violence may be quite different from the postulated goal achievement.

These questions are very relevant for future American social change, and it is clear that much more cross-fertilizatio is necessary between those who study America and those wh are concerned with politics and social change in developing areas. Furthermore, the study of the politics of violence mus be informed by the work of those concerned with personality and change. But there are already strong indications that work on personality and violence is going to treat violence as a pathological phenomenon much as work on insurgency treated guerrilla violence as a disease of a transitional period between tradition and modernity. There an understanding of violence as pathological behavior led to counterinsurgency responses. In the American context, thinking about violence may turn out to be dominated by therapeutic schools. The therapy to be applied may be directed at "sick people" who are violent or a "sick society" which harbors and causes violent behaviors. But we should take a hard look at this way of thinking about violence to see whether much is gained by it. It takes for granted that violence is somehow abnormal and may slide over the politics of violence—its social causes and consequences. The language of "sickness" and "therapy" may well turn out to be another set of clichés for obfuscating understanding, another way, to paraphrase Clifford Geertz (1968), of not wanting to learn too much about ourselves too quickly.

1. VIOLENCE IN THE GHETTO

*Violence is necessary and
it's as American as cherry pie.*

Rap Brown

In 1964, Harry Eckstein noted that social science had produced few studies on internal war/violent political disorder (Eckstein 1964, p. 1); earlier, Eckstein had noted the profusion of terms and terminological muddle for describing uses of violence in politics and had complained of a focus on guerrilla warfare—on the operational aspects of irregular warfare. Moreover, he pointed out that when analysts got around to the causes of internal wars they provided a plethora of hypotheses about causation. Treatment of the French Revolution was cited as a case in point: "Scarcely anything in the French *ancien régime* has not been blamed, by one writer or another, for the revolution" (Eckstein 1963, p. 20). Most propositions about internal war were structural rather than behavioral, i.e., about conditions rather than processes by which aggression is generated. Eckstein argued that we ought to be more concerned with attitudes and orientations than we had been formerly, particularly since so many conditions seemed able to generate internal war and since attitude patterns were seen to be to a large extent independent of objective conditions (pp. 47-52). What Eckstein called the behavioral approach would lead to the stressing of intellectual and voluntaristic factors in the etiology of political violence, rather than to the seeing of attitudes as more or less mechanical responses to specific conditions. In a word, Eckstein felt that the overabundance of hypotheses for internal war outbreak resulted from too little and the wrong kind of study of internal war (p. 20). (The French Revolution occurred because of too much or too little economic progress; too much or too little circulation of elites; the presence of conflicting social myths; too little social mobilization or anomie from excess mobilization; rapid social change; erratic social change; alienation of ruler and ruled; inefficient government; divisions among elites; and many more.)

We see in the writings on the outbreak of violence by Negroes in American cities many of the problems Eckstein referred to and some of the approaches he noted being debated. We also see the restatement of the "conventional wisdom" on insurgency in new states being applied to explain violence in the ghettos. For example, on multi-factor causation, an article in the *New York Times* of August 6, 1967 ("Psychiatrists Lay Negro Riots to Centuries-Old Social Stress"), gave the following reasons for rioting: Northern society was without social structure, rules, and emotional support for Negroes—the migration view. Negroes had reservoirs of hatred. There was loss of conscience and self-imposed control because of mass hysteria. There was a contagion of violence accentuated by the violence in American culture and its transmission through the mass media. Negroes themselves have a violent culture, having disrespect for law and order stemming from lynchings in the South and lack of impartial law enforcement in their neighborhoods. Negroes have been exposed to the brutalizing Big City Sickness, which dulls the senses, and they have discovered the falsehood of the dream that Big City Streets are paved with gold.

Negroes live in a matriarchal society and cannot develop self-esteem; they have self-destructive and suicidal impulses from a what-have-we-got-to-lose view. (These were cited by Dr. John P. Spiegel, director of the Lemberg Center for the Study of Violence at Brandeis.) By and large, these are what I suppose Eckstein would call behavioral factor causes rather than structural ones; obviously you can have an overabundance of the former as well as of the latter. The policy answers cited by Dr. Spiegel were contact with ghetto leaders and a police "mean"—not too much police violence or permissiveness. Dr. Alvin Poussaint reportedly gave a more structural answer in the same article: Break up the ghettos, provide more jobs and more political participation.

Bayard Rustin (1967) specifically replied to the question, "Don't the riots go further than economic underprivilege and the lack of jobs and are they not to be understood in terms of profound moral, cultural, and psychological factors—a feeling of powerlessness and identity crises?" by saying that there was a sense that the above was true but that it smacked of mystification. Rustin argued that Negroes' socioeconomic positions have not improved as much as had been imagined and in particular that they had not improved relatively. A position that goes further than Rustin's in stressing conditions rather than states of mind as causal factors for violence is that of Hodgkin—applied to Africa rather than America: "We should abandon also the tendency to substitute psychological for sociological categories of explanation. . . . It is not, primarily, the states of mind of individuals that need to be understood but the precise historical conditions which made it possible for these particular individuals, with their particular standpoints and attitudes, to emerge, and the character of the social movements in which they played a formative part and which at the same time helped to form them."

However, the "in" concept for explaining Negro rioting is, indeed, that of relative deprivation, rather than objectification of conditions themselves; thus the focus is on perception of conditions. William V. Shannon (1967*a, b*) cites statistics showing the increase in Negro college graduates, incomes, and legal decisions in Negroes' favor, and argues that in Detroit, at least, Negroes did participate in politics and shared power. He hearkens back to Alexis de Tocqueville's argument that improvement in conditions paradoxically brings about or contributes to violence. The unstable situation is the one beginning to improve; hopes are stirred where before there was only passivity and despair. Shannon echoes Crane Brinton when he argues that the dynamics of revolt work in favor of extremists. Reform begets more pressure. There are strains of a newer authority on revolution: Frantz Fanon. Shannon sees a small minority caught up in a romantic dream of ending all disabilities at one stroke: if the slum is an awful place, burn it down. He acknowledges (although he does not advocate) the cleansing force of violence which frees men from despair and feelings of inferiority, in Fanon's view. Shannon argues that, while repression of Negroes is one alternative for Americans, economic programs, on the other hand, will not suffice. This is because Negroes are demanding independence too. But no amount of violence can make Harlem or Mississippi an independent Negro Republic. What is the answer then? It is necessary to foster self-pride and community. It is necessary to foster a sense of nationhood— but is this possible without a nation?

Almost all observers of ghetto riots seem to agree that it is crucial to provide a sense of community. This means changing economic and social conditions for Negroes by bringing Negroes into urbanized, industrialized, modern America, ending the Two Nations, one of which is not even a nation. Negroes are seen as acting from personal motives because they are opting out of a political system in which they either have no weight or in which they are not being allowed to participate meaningfully (see Anthony Howard). Thus they want to share in symbols of material prosperity, argue those who point to the pattern of looting. Others, including Negro observers, note that secondhand junk stores were looted: bemoaned one Negro, "What kind of guys would go after that junk?"

If one chooses to focus on "conditions," it follows that massive attacks on the economic and social order are called for. If one emphasizes perceptions of conditions and introduces the concept of relative deprivation—a deprivation relative to where you were, where others are, where you think you ought to be—one must be aware of the possibility of more violence through betterment of conditions and a heightening of feelings of deprivation. If one chooses to emphasize the precipitants of violence and to see criminality pure and simple, calls for law enforcement are in order. (For a discussion of precipitants and conditions taken together see Lieberson and Silverman.) If one recognizes that violence may be necessary as a restorative of dignity and as an assertion of independence, and at the same time notes that the geographical base for independence is not available, one ought to confess to the difficulties and not try to slide over them as Shannon does.

Rustin is not in such difficulties, at least not consciously,
because he argues that if white blood was what rioters want-
ed, they did not go very far to get it; rather they assaulted the
symbols of white power: police and property. These are seen
by him as the traditional symbols of rebellions. For Rustin,
there are no preconditions for successful or even authentic
revolution of American Negroes on a nationalist basis, because the geography is not right and no popular majority is
struggling against a colonial minority. If the independence
revolutions are no model, what of social revolutions, where
revolution means to Rustin fundamental changes in social
and economic class relations, resulting from mass political
action? In America, such action would have to be, by definition—if it is to be mass—interracial. Thus for Rustin (1967)
Negroes can participate in such a revolution, or provoke
counterrevolution, but they cannot bring revolution about
by themselves. This is clearly opposed to a view heard at the
Chicago Convention on New Politics: We will liberate you
despite yourselves. It is also opposed to the advocates of
Black Power who define a situation where Negroes are already in rebellion, on the verge of revolution, moving into
a state of guerrilla war and moving from violence against
other Negroes to violence against whites.

Rustin's argument is essentially an argument about the
nature of potentialities of classes when he moves from the
impossibility of an independence revolution to a social revolution of and by and for Negroes. Not just numbers are
at stake. The class content is wrong for an exclusively Negro
social revolution. Negroes constitute a lower class, not a
working class; a lumpenproletariat, not a proletariat. The unemployed and the marginally unemployed are unorganized

and unstable and contain petty-criminal and antisocial elements. Can such a social stratum be the central agent of historical transformation? The answer has been no. A traditional argument is being applied here to the potentiality for Negro revolution. Many voices have been raised arguing that
revolution is no longer possible in the City, or in cities, or in
industrial areas, or in industrial countries, because too much
force can be brought to bear against insurrection in cities;
because cities are themselves parasitical and bourgeois vis-à-
vis the countryside (the Sierra versus the Llano); because
there are no longer meaningful social splits in industrial countries; because revolutions happen in transitional periods when
nation-building processes are in initial traumatic stages of
breakdown without new consolidation, and new loyalties
and policies are not yet established. We shall look at these
views below. Here I mean only to point out that Rustin's argument rests on the absence of the right class, or more precisely, the inability of Negroes to substitute for a proletariat,
to make a social revolution.

    For Rustin, violence exists in the ghettos because the con-
ditions of life are the fuse of violence, incidents are the match,
and the powderkeg is the social background of the individual.
Riots become riotous manifestations of rebellion; they are
more than riots but less than politically coherent rebellions.
Rustin's answer is to try and create a true social revolution
with an alliance of Negroes and other groups which will fuse
into a real working class. Coalitions and new major ties are
required. Whether this new class might carry out its revolution with violence or might provoke violent counterrevolution, Rustin does not tell us. The implication he leaves is
that Negro violence is to be channeled into coalition politics:

this will prove efficacious for policy and will also give political participation which will bring direct ameliorative results.

Carmichael and Hamilton focus on the conditions which lead to violence, in much the same way that Rustin does. They, too, describe the conditions which create dynamite in the ghettos and they see explosions of frustration, despair, and hopelessness. For them the match which ignites the dynamite is the ineptness of decision-makers and the anachronistic institutions which inhibit innovation. Thus their precipitants of violence are not specific incidents but institutionalized white racism (pp. 160-62). For Carmichael and Hamilton, the initiative for needed change must come from the black community, which must be the base of organization to control institutions in that community. There is no emphasis in Carmichael and Hamilton's book that the new political forms they call for will channel black violence into "constructive" paths. Rather, they put forward Black Power as a political framework and ideology which is the "last reasonable opportunity for this society to work out its racial problems short of prolonged destructive guerrilla warfare." Participation in the decision-making process will bring returns; at the same time, participation in decisions and control of institutions will bring attachment to institutions. But Black Power is not therapy; it is a political substitute for guerrilla warfare insofar as it can provide a means "whereby a new politicized people can get what they need from the government" (p. 18

Lewis Coser provides us with a strategy similar to Rustin although it rests upon a more elaborate sociological underpinning. In *The Functions of Social Conflict* (1956), Coser deals with the integrative aspects of conflict rather than with violence specifically. In fact, Coser maintains that Sorel's advocacy of "violence" is to be understood entirely in terms of Sorel's awareness of the close relationship between conflict and group cohesion. Only if the working class engaged in warfare with the middle class could it preserve its distinctive social character. Through action, members became aware of class identity. For Marx too, class constitutes itself only through conflict. Coser takes up Simmel's famous proposition that even in entering into violent relationships, the very act of conflict establishes a relationship where none may have been before. Thus violence may be a binding element between parties that may have stood in no relationship before, and where violence is more than an attack of the thug upon his victim, conflict gives rise to rules and regulations and to norms governing the conduct of restraining of violence. The Coser-Simmel-derived propositions stress the integrating, balance-of-power maintaining, and creative aspects of conflict. But what of overt violence which may fracture norms, which may rise out of increasing participation in politics? How much, where, and at what juncture is violence rather than conflict functional for society's integration?

Coser, in another work (1966), turned some attention to these questions, but we ought not to take leave of *The Functions of Social Conflict* without first noting that values had to be shared beforehand or shared values had to be created during the process of conflict (But how? And why sometimes but not at other times?) for conflict not to be disruptive. In "Internal Violence as a Mechanism for Conflict Resolution" Coser saw violence as serving social structures by furnishing mechanisms for conflict-resolution when established authority fails to accommodate to demands of new groups for hearings. (Kornhauser [1964, p. 142], too, has seen rebellions as ways of making demands on authority—whether for changes in rulers, or in structures, or for specific acts.) Coser takes it to be axiomatic that men, other than those trained in legitimate or illegitimate use of violence, will resort to violent action only under extremely frustrating, ego-damaging, and anxiety-provoking conditions. (We might point out that this kind of formulation would be more useful if there were some criteria for these states aside from the fact of violence. The proposition is tautological, and Coser admits it when he says he takes this as axiomatic, but the language implies something more than axioms. Furthermore, what we want to know is why some men do train for the illegitimate use of violence, since we often call these men revolutionaries.)

Coser believes that when men turn to violence they are rejecting the use of a political community and that when they commit violence or even threaten it, psychic energy is required. True, for a man to join a small group in the jungle requires commitment, but does joining a street riot? Or a pogrom? It may be the thing to do and may show real social solidarity. Coser also maintains that since violence testifies to great frustration and serious commitment it is likely to be perceived by those in power as a serious indicator of maladjustment. We have any number of *anciens régime* that did not so perceive or did not act on their perceptions or did not act in a way to alleviate maladjustments, but at least some are in the first category, failure to perceive. Coser believes that the perception of violence by rulers can lead to remedial social action for those who commit violence.

Acts of violence are for him often highly instrumental and realistic acts. Indeed, Coser sees abject adjustment to suffering as indicating a sense of reality as impaired as that of persons who commit violent acts whom we call chiliasts. Coser has a place for nonrealistic conflicts, but these are occasioned not by rival ends of the antagonists but by needs for tension release for one of them. We should note that there are those who argue, after Fanon, that tension release can be thought of not as unrealistic or merely expressive but as leading to a new state of mind and to new action for individuals and social groups.

Coser is primarily replying to the view that ghetto riots are senseless, a view held even by some who admit the importance of high unemployment, inadequate schools, dilapidated housing, etc., and who see these conditions as setting the stage for the riots. These conditions were all noted by the McCone Report, which nonetheless concluded that "the rioters seem to have been caught up in an insensate rage of destruction." Rustin (1966), Blauner, and Coser (1966) saw the ghetto riots as a call for help and attention which stemmed most directly from a failure to get a political hearing. Blauner saw Watts as an attempt to get control over the community. Thus political power as well as political participation is stressed.

Perhaps Coser's most interesting point is one which goes beyond seeing the riots as signals of discontent and attempts to alter power balances. For he recognized that for many there seemed to be no other means available; that is, there seemed no possibility for considering alternatives to riots. For Coser, this is nonrealistic behavior. Behavior wherein there is no conceivable alternative to destructive violence—

as it appears in its purest form, e. g. lynchings—is behavior where the acting-out becomes an end in itself. But once again we must raise Fanon, who sees the committing of violent acts as therapeutic. Coser has a social-structural explanation for this kind of violence: Negroes in general and the Watts community in particular do not participate in a pluralistic society—in a pattern of cross-cutting groups. Thus Negroes fight in an unsegmented struggle; lack of participation in a multiplicity of groups leads to intense and bitter conflicts. The total involvement of personality and the accumulation of suppressed hostilities increase the intensity, and the more intense the conflict, the higher the chances of admixtures of nonrealistic elements into what may, at origin, have been realistic behavior. For Coser, the incidence of political violence in modern, industrial societies of the West has been successfully minimized because excluded groups are themselves rare; channels typically exist for the assertion of groups within a framework of political legitimacy. Modernity is a state of open channels of political communication, and so you get little political violence in it. Violence comes about when groups cannot get heard or when some groups feel they have a vested interest in suppressing voices being raised and resort to violence rather than opening up the political structure. For Coser, the one group in a Western industrial society that is not getting a hearing is the American Negro group. But this is not true, strictly speaking. There are other groups that do not get a hearing—Mexicans, American Indians, and certain regionally defined poor whites—and this has been recognized by an unidentified member of the President's National Advisory Commission on Civil Disorders, who was quoted as saying: "The race problem is the core. The poverty problem is something we have to face. But we can't say it is the cause of riots. There are many other poor groups in the country—whites, Indians, Mexicans—but they don't riot" (*New York Times*, February 25, 1968).

In the Coser analysis, public and private policy can affect patterns of violence by opening up the system. Since active minorities who engage in violence cannot be ignored, even when they are small (and 10 percent of the population, centered either in cities or a few states is not small), it is rational for the wider society to make some accommodation with the violent group. What is left out is the nature of the accommodation, the costs of accommodation against the costs of further violence, and the possibility of "irrational" response to rational violence. But above all, what is questionable is Coser's axiom that men resort to violence only under extreme conditions—when we do not know what such conditions consist of and for whom. This is the more troublesome proposition, since men have resorted to violence very often to achieve political and other ends. Thus, even if one treats conflict and violence as functional so that stability and violence may go together, the frequency of violence must be accounted for, and explanations must be made of the behavior of groups committing violent acts.

As was noted above, analysts of Negro violence have stressed the conditions of ghetto life or a set of attitudes associated with those conditions but not mechanistically derived from them. Race is treated as being relevant because Negroes as a group happen to have a large majority associated with a particular set of social and economic conditions. But the importance of race can be asserted in different ways.

It has been maintained that Negroes have a propensity for violence simply because they are Negroes. National-character or "biological" arguments have been made, although these are not necessarily the same kinds of analyses. One could argue, for example, that although other groups are poor, do not get a hearing, and suffer from social ills, they do not resort to violence because of some presumed biological or cultural factor operating. Of course, it is possible to be specific about race in nonbiological terms by spelling out what is meant by culture. For example, Glazer and Moynihan write about the impact of a matriarchal family structure, which itself can be understood in historical, social, and economic terms. Janowitz has said that the history of the Negro has been markedly different from that of other immigrant and minority groups. Race for Janowitz is shorthand for a complex of historical factors which produce racial situations. Race is treated as a variable understood to be linked to other variables, but not in independent-dependent relationships. Rather, race must be understood in terms of the interaction effect of a number of variables.

Race can also be treated as a "truly" independent variable in that a specific kind of blood tie which links a community can be singled out as the critical factor. One could complicate this by taking into account the size of the community, its leadership, and other things about it as well as the normative or biological principles by which they are linked. In studies that refer to racial violence, racial hostility between groups is salient. The analysts might agree that social and economic factors are at work in this hostility, but at a given level of analysis it is the antagonism of the groups themselves to which attention is called. Studies

abound of ethnic violence or tribal violence as well as racial
violence in America, in these terms. Janowitz calls this "communal" violence, or "contested area" violence (pp. 9-10).
This is ecological warfare because it involves a direct struggle
between white and Negro areas. Communal violence is a term
which emphasizes the feelings and the cognitions that groups
have about each other, and the groups' reactions to each
other. These feelings are important not only in triggering
and sustaining violence; the history of violence between racial groups sets precedents for violence and conditions expectations about future violence.

In the absence of surveys which tell us specifically who
is rioting over periods of time—that is, from riot to riot—it
is difficult to say precisely in what direction the precedents
work. Janowitz says that "the participants in riots are likely
to be persons who have taken part in previous outbursts"
(p. 19). Yet on a previous page, Janowitz, in making an interesting point about the mass media, says, "It is as if the
rioters learned the lesson emphasized in the mass media, that
mass destruction achieves no tangible benefit"; and, "It also
appears that there is a social learning process for both the
Negro community and for the larger society when a mass
riot takes place, which inhibits the repetition of another
similar outburst" (p. 18). Janowitz notes that television has
served as the main instrument for impressing the realities of
the riots onto the mass consciousness of the nation; he argues that television has been important in exacerbating tensions and furthering the "contagion-of-riot" effect and that
images presented tend to reinforce predispositions to participate and even to legitimate participation in violence. But
in terms of his social learning theory one might expect an

argument to be made that television inhibits future riots by
facilitating a learning process about the lack of tangible benefits from mass rioting. Perhaps there is only an apparent
contradiction. If the time factor is made clear, an argument
can be advanced that television enforces a short-term contagion effect during riots and inhibits future riots when a
longer time span is considered. Furthermore, what may be
true for a large population—that predispositions to violence
are lessened by participation in riots and observation of them
on television—may not be true for a smaller population which
participates again but in a more organized way.

Janowitz himself focuses on a shift to more specific, more
premeditated, and more regularized uses of force. Violence
becomes political violence or political terror. The mass media
may lead some individuals disposed to violence to use violence
in a more organized way and to move toward political violence
as they perceive the lack of results from mass rioting. It is difficult to see how a number of competing hypotheses along
these lines could be confirmed or denied without research
concerned with participants in mass rioting and membership
in political organizations that espouse violence. The latter is
necessary also to come to grips with the Janowitz argument
that the use of violence supplies a new power base in the Negro community. Violent activities, he says, increase and become institutionalized; they also expand into new realms
(p. 19). (The National Advisory Committee on Civil Disorders has done surveys on rioters and nonrioters in Newark
and Detroit which do provide profiles of rioters.)

Racial violence during World War I and after and, for example, in Detroit in 1943, involved fighting between whites
and Negroes; it was communal violence. But the riots in

Watts in 1965 and in Newark and Detroit in 1967 did not involve direct conflict on a major scale between contending whites and blacks except insofar as white authorities who tried to repress violence were on hand or white shopkeepers were targets. But even in the latter instance it was the shops, not the shopkeepers, which were involved since their owners lived outside the ghetto. A number of arguments have come to grips with the fact that large-scale violence has been within the ghetto. There are those who argue that Negroes commit violence within the ghetto because they cannot get, physically, to white areas. Since great distances are not involved between the ghetto and white areas—that is, there is a border area at hand—this argument must rest on police ability to cordon off the ghetto at the start of a riot. Janowitz says that law-enforcement officers increased their capacity to contain and repress communal violence. Yet the obvious inability of the police to contain rioting within the ghetto in 1965 and 1967, and in particular the initial paralysis of the police at the start of rioting, makes one doubtful that control mechanisms *prevented* violence from moving outside the ghettos, although the police did move to cordon off areas and hold a fallback position at the edge of the ghetto. Tom Hayden has asserted that in Newark the spread of violence was in the hands of the people rather than of the police (p. 15).

The Fanon argument applied to the ghetto is that violence is turned inward against self because the true target group cannot be got at for fear of repression and because of psychological reluctance to attack this group. Hate therefore turns inward. A modified Fanon argument is that, since the ghetto both symbolizes and is concretely all that is

hateful, it is burned down as a spontaneous act. Then we
have the Two Nations argument of Howard and many others,
which stresses a desire to go after the symbols of material
prosperity. Janowitz calls the 1965 and 1967 riots "commodity riots," since the outbursts, including looting, were against
property and retail establishments (p. 10). Hayden says that
schools and banks were not attacked, although they were perceived to be oppressive institutions, because their buildings
contained little that could be carried off. "To this extent the
Newark riot was concrete rather than symbolic" (p. 18).
Edward Schneier has made the interesting suggestion to me
that Negro looting might be seen as an apolitical means of
economic advancement—as an attempt to redistribute income without going through a modernizing process. Alter-
nately, Schneier suggests, violence may be seen as a weapon
of those who oppose modernization if it is to take place
without a full-scale revolution.

Janowitz' understanding of the movement from communal violence to commodity violence is essentially an
ecological one. Racial warfare is minimized because areas
of Negro population concentration rise. Thus "as Negro
enclaves develop in suburban areas, forms of communal
riots between Negroes and whites become a reality in these
areas for the first time" (Janowitz, p. 18). Since it is not
likely that social tensions will decline drastically in the next
years, whatever the improvements in the socioeconomic position of Negroes, the spread of Negroes outside the ghetto
might well transform rioting once again into communal
rioting. Janowitz suggests that already the mass riot "commodity" pattern is being transformed to a more organized
and political one as both law-enforcement institutions and

elements in the Negro population learn to modify their behavior.

Janowitz' essay, presented at the end of 1967, takes up a major theme of violence in American urban areas—the role of the instruments of social control: the police and military forces. It is not a new idea to stress the role of instruments for suppressing violence in the outbreak, duration, and scope of violence. Nineteenth-century socialists argued that violence came about when a power structure reacted with violence to demands for change in the system. Marx's arguments for the necessity of violence in social change were based on an understanding of the reactions of ruling classes and then the subsequent response of challenging classes. In discussions of precipitants of violence, police brutality is often stressed as an instigator of violence. But prior to specific police actions against individuals and groups is a community perception of the police as a tool of direct intimidation, harassment, and violence. As Hayden has said, ". . . the Police Department was seen as the spearhead of organized hostility to Negro action, an armed unit protecting the privileges of the shrinking white community of the city" (p. 14). In his anatomy of violence in Newark, Hayden documents the growth of police violence during riots. Moreover, he argues, the troops called in were used to patrol aggressively against people inside the ghetto rather than to prevent looting (p. 19). In this connection, it may be that recent violence in the ghetto can be seen, in part, as a response to the fact that the police have only just begun to try to penetrate the ghetto, whereas they have left it alone in the past.

Among sociologists and political scientists, Allen Grimshaw has provided some of the most interesting work

concerned with analyzing the role of the police in racial violence. One of Grimshaw's major propositions is that color
violence (or what Janowitz calls communal violence) "is a
consequence not of conscious policy decisions but results
rather from reactions by the dominant group to real or perceived assaults upon the status quo within a context of var-
iation of attitude and action in agencies of external control"
(Grimshaw 1962). It follows that in order to understand cases
of color violence we must have a prior understanding of the
nature of the accommodative structure and of the different
assaults on it. Grimshaw undertakes to analyze violence in the
North and South, and in different specific riots, in a number
of essays, to make comparisons of accommodative structures
and the nature of violence. This enables him both to be more
analytical about precipitants of violence than is often the case
when commentators list the many specific actions that may
lead to generalized violence—e.g., turning off fire hydrants
when children are at play, giving a traffic ticket, etc.—and to
cut away from a focus on precipitants of violence to come to
grips with a total social situation.

Grimshaw sees precipitants of violence in the South as violations of what are called sacred spheres of valued and established patterns. These are violations of doctrines of white su-
premacy; for example, the transgressions which are particularly reacted against are slurs against whites, rapes, lack of def-
erence. Tensions in the North after World War I took place
in the secular sphere of jobs, housing, and transportation, as
Negroes migrated to new areas. Yet, Grimshaw says, the background factors of prejudice, discrimination, and social tension
(what others would call the conditions for violence) are present in all urban centers in the North with a relatively or

absolutely great Negro population in a degree sufficient to permit the development of situations characterized by "violence-process." Thus, "the eruption or non-eruption of internal violence is determined . . . by the character of external forces of constraint and control, especially the police forces" (Grimshaw 1962).

Grimshaw (1963a) has also said that "there is no direct relation between the level of social tension and the eruption of social violence." As Janowitz points out, because of the complex meaning of the term "no direct relation" it is not necessary to accept all that this proposition implies. "It is enough to reemphasize the obvious fact that in the United States, social tension exists where riots break out, and to accept his [Grimshaw's] alternative formulation that 'in every case where major rioting has occurred, the social structure of the community has been characterized by weak patterns of external control' " (Janowitz, p. 7, citing Grimshaw 1963b). Grimshaw, then, takes tension levels for granted, which is, as we shall see, quite different from the attempts to find causal factors for violence by trying to measure levels of tension—either qualitatively, as in much of the work on violence, or quantitatively, as in some of the newer theories of civil violence, e.g., Gurr's.

Grimshaw has admitted that his major proposition, that the eruption of violence depends on the character of external forces of control, needs testing. Yet one has a feeling of *déjà vu* in reading the report of the United States Congress, House of Representatives Social Committee authorized by Congress to investigate the East St. Louis riots of 1918, and other reports that Grimshaw (1963b) reproduces. These excoriate the police and troops used in riot situations, as Hayden and the Report of the President's National Advisory Commission on Civil Disorders do. But whereas the President's Advisory Commission found that the major difference between the riots of Newark and Detroit and many other disturbances effectively suppressed was the manner in which "the police and responsible leaders responded to the initial incident," Grimshaw and Hayden see the police not as neutral arbiters of social disputes but as armed representatives of the communities from which they were originally recruited; moreover, this perception, Grimshaw says, is shared by white and Negro communities and by the police themselves. (Treatment of the primary importance of agencies of external control can also be found in Grimshaw [1963*c*].)

Richard Lambert has also examined the relationship between communal violence and external controls in observations of violence in India. As Grimshaw points out, no American city, with the possible exception of Chicago, which has had frequent racial skirmishes as well as some major violence, has had continuous riots over a number of years, as have some Indian cities. Five of Lambert's propositions are reproduced here as an illustration of the kinds of propositions that need testing in relating social controls to violence. (That those who are concerned with formulating propositions about social control as well as those engaged in formulating propositions about social conditions and levels of tension may be engaged in creating contradictory hypotheses can be seen by comparing Lambert's points one and five.)

1.   A highly visible display of overwhelming force at command of government decreases likelihood of violence.

2.   In absence of such power, patterns of social con-
     trol rather than objective strength of force is the
     important factor:
     a. the longer the time required to visibly domi-
        nate the situation, the greater the likelihood
        of violence;
     b. the greater the susceptibility of civil government
        to public criticism, the greater the likelihood of
        violence;
     c. the greater the degree of violence in process of
        suppression (harsher aggression), the less the
        likelihood of violence;
     d. the greater the uniformity of application of con-
        trol, the less the likelihood of violence;
     e. the greater the comprehensiveness and harshness
        of punishment after disturbances, the less the
        probability of future violence.
3.   The more frequently a pattern or agency of govern-
     ment control is used, the less effective becomes its
     deterrent value.
4.   In the face of increasing numbers of riots stability
     can be restored by:
     a. increasing the strength of the forces;
     b. varying one or more of the elements in the con-
        trol pattern.
5.   In the use of forces to control riots, increments in
     force are more important than the initial engage-
     ment of superior forces.
          [Grimshaw 1963*b*, p. 284, citing Lambert]

When social control mechanisms are treated in isolation

from a wider social context, discussions about effective patterns of social control become arid. This has happened in much of the writing on counterinsurgency as well as in works devoted to violence in America. This criticism does not apply to Grimshaw, who shares Hayden's perception of the police as an instrument of social control by a dominant group. He sees a solution to violence only in changes in attitudes of members of the dominant group. Nonetheless, the tactics, organization, and recruitment policies of police agencies matter to him. Janowitz has built on Grimshaw's work and elaborated an idea of "social control of escalated riots." For Janowitz, both organizational weakness and professional limitations of law-enforcement agencies and a moral and social climate that encourages violence are among the elements that account for the outbreak of mass rioting (p. 7).

Janowitz argues that weakness in the system of social control must be understood in terms of a wide range of institutions: the family, the school, religious organizations, and voluntary associations as well as police agencies, the mass media, and the widespread availability of weapons. He proposes a domestic disarmament which goes well beyond technical problems in the management of violence as he elaborates an idea of the constabulary which is an effort to base the practices of law-enforcement agencies on fundamental political and moral commitments. The emphasis is on a selective response to violence and concern with minimum applications of force (p. 26). But Janowitz, too, writes about effective patterns of social control without asking: whose control?

Before turning to work which has tried to explain why industrial societies are comparatively free of political violence and to a body of literature which examines violence in nonindustrialized societies, we note that in March, 1968, the aforementioned National Advisory Commission on Civil Disorders published the text of its summary report (*New York Times*, March 1, 1968). (Later the complete text was published.) This document is both a micropolitical account of incidents occurring in specific riots and a sweeping call for action based on a particular understanding of violence. The Commission asserts that violence cannot build a better society. "Disruption and disorder nourish repression, not justice." This assertion runs counter to the views of many revolutionaries, past and present. In addressing the question, "Why did it happen?" the National Advisory Commission says that the factors are complex and vary significantly in their effect from city to city and from year to year; the consequences of one disorder become the causes of the next. Yet, the Commission says, a primary factor can be pointed to: "White racism is essentially responsible for the explosive mixture which has been accumulating in our cities since the end of World War II." Specifically, white terrorism—the response of the dominant structure—is singled out, and the police are identified with this response. While the National Advisory Commission notes frustrated hopes (relative deprivation?) and outlines the conditions of ghetto life, the focus is less on the perceptions of Negroes and measuring changes in conditions than on the response of a power structure to an out-group's demands. This is an emphasis that is not present in much of the current writing on revolution and counterinsurgency, which tends to focus on the insurgents and their social and economic environment without specifying the nature of the authority structures they confront and try to

change, and the actions and responses of authorities to insurgency.

The *Report of the National Advisory Commission on
Civil Disorders* puts itself forward as a document based on
hasty but intensive study of a number of cases. It does not
examine at length all the assumptions contained within it
about violence. Nor does it attempt to specify consequences
and costs of violence as well as causes. It takes for granted
deleterious effects. Moreover, the Commission's task was
not to use its understanding of violence in urban America to
formulate a theory of violence and social change which would
try to generalize causes and consequences of violence. The
Report was designed to meet a social crisis and to provide
therapy, in the sense of aiming to alleviate social conditions
with specific recommendations, to speak to a white conscience, and to tell black Americans "We understand." Indeed, much of the writing on violence in America and in developing areas is designed to be therapeutic. This does not
mean that those concerned with therapy cannot make contri-
butions to our understanding of violence. It usually has meant
however, that concerns with violence have been very specific
ones. Moreover, if violence is to be treated therapeutically,
it is understood as being pathological even if violence may be
"a good thing" for the afflicted patient or society.

There are exceptions to this criticism, and it may be that
studies of violence in America are moving away from this
kind of analysis. Whatever the weaknesses in Carmichael and
Hamilton's work (and Christopher Lasch has made telling
points about its failure to pursue any line of reasoning
through to its conclusion, including its insistence on black
community organization), *Black Power* is one example of

a movement away from treating violence as either pathologically bad or romantically good. Another example is Harold Cruse's *The Crisis of the Negro Intellectual.* Cruse does not confuse violent protest with fundamental social change. The espousing of and participation in violent action is not *ipso facto* radical for him. Lasch (p. 12), commenting on Cruse's work, notes that many black militants have seen "armed self-defense" as a form of revolutionary action. But, Lasch argues, "The issue of armed self-defense does not touch the deep-rooted conditions that have to be changed if the Negro's position is to be changed." Lasch associates himself with Cruse's view that "violence becomes a meaningful strategy only insofar as American institutions resist radical change and resist it violently." And, "since the Negro movement has not yet even formulated a program for radical change, violence is tactically premature." When Cruse says that "the main front of tactics must always be organizational and institutional," his understanding of the place of violence as a tactic of social change is much closer to Lenin's and Mao's ideas than to those of Debray. For Cruse has avoided treating violence per se and insists on separating out violence and social change by asking about the consequences for change of violent politics on the part of specific actors at given points in time.

As we turn now to studies of guerrilla war, revolution, and totalitarianism, we bear in mind the fundamental distinction between those who do or do not consider violence to be *ipso facto* a radical act as long as it is violence against a repressive system. We will try to see at what points these analyses meet understandings of violence in America and how they link violence and modernization.

2. GUERRILLA WAR

> *To conquer is to accept as*
> *a matter of principle that*
> *life, for the revolutionary,*
> *is not the supreme good.*
>   Regis Debray

The citation from Debray does not flatly contradict the proposition that men will resort to violence only under extreme conditions. It says nothing about extreme conditions, only that something is more important than life for the revolutionary and that he undertakes insurrection to achieve it. Those who have concerned themselves with revolution gener—violence and guerrilla war specifically—ask: Why do violence and internal war occur? The focus in the literature on guerrilla wars has largely been on the wars themselves—the tactics of fighting them. Increasingly, a concern is raised with prevention of guerrilla wars, particularly since prevention is seen as the best tactic, given the military difficulties involved in winning against guerrillas. Less often, there is concern with the outcomes of guerrilla wars.

Great revolutions have been discussed in terms of the persistence of old traditions or in terms of radical change; rarely have contemporary guerrilla struggles been analyzed for outcomes beyond a calculus of winner and loser. Levy (1967) for one, suggests that insurgents may be defeated yet nonetheless transform the social structure in the direction they desire or in some other direction. The proposition that insurgents may win but not transform society, since the old society persists, has been evident in writing on revolution and in writing on coups. The significance of Levy's work here is that some types of internal wars may have determinate concrete outcomes, no matter who wins them in a conventional sense (Eckstein 1963, p. 28). But there has been, on the whole, relatively little recent work of this kind and very little examination of outcomes for social change in societies which have recently had guerrilla wars, e.g., Malaya, Algeria, Philippines, and North Vietnam.

Clausewitz, however, saw that some social groups had the same enemy as guerrillas in national independence struggles but would nonetheless be against guerrilla war because it was dangerous to the social order. There was implicit in his writings the idea that guerrilla war was per se revolutionary and transforming because of the way in which guerrilla wars were fought. They are fought not through established elites and they bring physical disruption. Political problems *may* exist for any order when government arms civilians for a foreign struggle. But wars fought on home soil are transforming. Insurrectionists usually are concerned with change in specific directions. Revolutionaries have in mind social changes and redistributions of power; those who promulgate coups want to replace the "ins" with themselves. Even jacqueries want an end to things, sometimes to specific taxes, at other times to "injustice" (Hobsbawm). Traditional groups may want a return to the past. The point is that goals are at hand. Groups do not commit violence animated by the view that society needs a change, any change, and that all that counts is that violence will work toward transforming society. Some individuals may join violent movements with such views in mind, but they do not characterize the movement as a whole.

It may be fair to say that the bulk of the work on guerrilla war, including the contemporary "classics" by revolutionaries Mao, Guevara, Giap, and Debray, has been more

concerned with techniques of violence appropriate to stages
of insurrection than with outcomes for social change, althoug[
implicitly there is much in these writings suggestive for consi[
ering outcomes. Works on counterinsurgency (Osanka, Wolfe,
Pustay, Greene) have been concerned largely with tactics of
fighting guerrillas. The proponents of guerrilla war take large[
for granted the reasons for the war's beginning. The war is an
outcome of revolutionary struggle against an unjust and historically doomed regime. The organic tie between people and
army or people's army is also assumed. At the least, the tie
must be forged for success to be gained. Once it is forged,
success will be gained, although there may be trials and tribu-
lations. Interest in the works cited above centers on the place
of the army itself. Writers on counterinsurgency see many
causes of the outbreak of insurrection. But they often stress
the difficulty in responding to insurgency via social and economic improvement programs during a military upheaval. We
will briefly illustrate these points.

For Mao, war and politics are inseparable; war is the politics of bloodshed. Of special interest to us here are the following of Mao's views: The people will rise in protest even
if leaders make compromises with oppressors. War experi-
ences are of a special kind. Those who take part in them mus[
rid themselves of ordinary habits and accustom themselves to
war before they can win victory. The army is not the instrument of the state but its spirit. "For eighteen years the development, consolidation, and Bolshevization of our Party
have been inseparable from guerrilla war" (from *Guerrilla
Warfare Is the Inevitable Path*, in Schram, p. 257). Yet Mao's
writings on guerrilla war have been analyzed for their relevance to contemporary potential guerrilla wars more than

for their relevance to the present organization of the Chinese
Communist party and society.

Debray, too, focused on the importance of the revolutionary army per se. The revolutionary is forged out of fighting
(*Revolution in the Revolution?*). In fact, Debray goes further
than Mao. For where Mao stresses the ebb and flow of the
guerrilla war and stages of advance and retreat, Debray stresses staking all through revolutionary action. "Guerrilla warfare is to peasant uprising what Marx is to Sorel" (p. 29). The
point here is to relate violence and uprising to change—change
in the mentality of those who struggle above all. Insurrection
is a total political strategy for total change. True, Debray
shows a concern for principles of military movement and technical matters. Guerrillas should not have a tactic of undertaking
decisive battles that can cost them the revolution (pp. 57-58).
But Debray does not mean that the revolution can really be
lost even through poor tactics; it can be delayed. On the other
hand, "To risk all means that, having risen in the mountains,
the fighters must wage a war to the death, a war that does not
admit of truces, retreats, compromises." Through this kind of
struggle, a rebel army is formed which is ideologically proletar-
ian. The posing of Sierra versus Llano implies an opposition of
forces even after rebel victory. The Sierra army has become revolutionary through guerrilla warfare. And here the kind of
violence seems important. Not acts of terrorism in the cities,
but the fighting of armed columns in the rural areas, is the
kind of violence that forges the revolutionary army. Nor can
Debray's point be seen as a stress on social mobilization of the
rural area. For the Cuban experience was not that. Large numbers of peasants were not mobilized on the Chinese model.
The guerrilla *focos* that Debray argues should be set up in

South America are not the large-scale-administered territories of China during the prolonged war but guerrilla bands existing without being centered in populated areas. This makes sense in light of Debray's emphasis on army rather than peasantry and on revolutionary rather than mass movement.

For Mao, a war of resistance against a domestic and foreign enemy required national mobilization. True, organized peasant violence was essential. Unorganized violence of the peasant jacqueries, of Razin and Pugachev, fails. (See Mao's *The Bitter Sufferings of the Peasants in Kiangsu and Chekiang and Their Movements of Resistance,* in Schram, pp. 178-79.) For Mao, rural revolution is an act of violence whereby one class overthrows the authority of another. Peasants have to use maximum strength to overthrow the deeply rooted authority of the landlords. Here violence implies a rooting out of habitual patterns, a cleansing of the slate for the peasant as well as perhaps more importantly, the physical and social elimination of the landlord class. "The rural areas must experience a great, fervent, revolutionary upsurge, which alone can arouse hundreds of thousands of people to form a great force." Violence implicates and involves people. (See Mao's *An Analysis of the Various Classes of the Chinese Peasantry and Their Attitudes toward Revolution*, in Schram, pp. 172-77.) Furthermore it is through being a target of terror, a recipient of violence, that a class becomes strong. The Chinese proletariat is seen as being more resolute and thoroughgoing in the revolutionary struggle because it has been most subjected to oppression by imperialism, the bourgeoisie, and feudal forces—and in China with a ruthlessness and severity seldom found in other nations. (Mao's *The Particular Characteristics of the Chinese Peasantry and the Chinese Proletariat*, in Schram, pp. 189-92.)

Reflecting that Bertrand Russell had argued in a lecture in Changsha in 1920 that education could be employed to change the consciousness of propertied classes, that communism without dictatorship could come about, Mao argued that this was not feasible historically and psychologically. That is, propertied classes did not change in this manner, and oppressed classes themselves required this kind of struggle. Thus the need for violence in a period of dictatorship, albeit in the Maoist scheme a brief reign of terror was necessary to suppress activities of counterrevolutionaries and to establish authority of the formerly oppressed—to establish it for and to themselves. Mao's concern for the use of violence in building the new man can be seen also in his view of economy of force. In dealing with the enemy, one must struggle savagely and attack mercilessly, but to do this with comrades is a mistake. A false show of authority whereby cadres try to instill terror in followers is both useless and pernicious. To transform the consciousness of the masses, "We absolutely must not proceed by orders or constraints" (from *Against the Intimidation of Comrades,* in Schram, p. 216). Similarly, soldiers should behave not like bandits but as representatives of a new social and economic order, not only because the former would prove counterproductive in the countryside but because it would demoralize soldiers themselves.

Violence in general, then, and not merely guerrilla terror, is a social weapon only to be used against certain targets for specified reasons. These reasons are not tactical; that is, they are not primarily framed out of a fear that uncontrolled violence will antagonize peasants. Rather, the reasons relate to a conception of violence used for self-transformation as well as for class victory. And Mao's concern is with the fundamental transformation of individuals —the creation of new men.

Lenin, too, has expressed similar views in his *Partisan Warfare* (1962). The American editors of this piece see it as a call for terrorism, or Blanquism (p. 66). But Lenin harnessed his ideas about violence to a conception of social change, or more accurately, for him violence and social change were inseparable under certain conditions. For Lenin, if the Party takes partisan actions into its own hands, if it directs violence, then violence will not, cannot, demoralize workers. For Lenin, the aggravation of political crises and growing pauperization, famine, and unemployment led to armed combat. In the early twentieth century in Russia, déclassé elements of the population, the lumpenproletariat and anarchist groups, chose armed struggle as the only form of social warfare. This was mistaken but does not compromise all forms of violence, argued Lenin.

What Mao, Debray, and Lenin are getting at is that under conditions of a specifiable kind, well-organized violence is the shortest distance between two points (as Trotsky once said it *always* seemed to Stalin).

Before taking up social-science theorists of guerrilla war and counterinsurgency, it may be useful to mention two contemporary theorists of insurrection who are often dismissed as being mere parrots of Mao: Giap and Guevara.

Like Mao, Vo Nguyen Giap, in *People's War, People's Army,* stresses social mobilization through guerrilla war and then a passing on to a different stage of army struggle. There is perhaps a less muted theme of selective terror in Giap. One

point worth noting is Giap's insistence that in the final stage
of the strategic offensive the one condition for success is the
regularization and modernization of the army itself. This is
a military necessity. The stress is on the transformation of
the instrument of violence which now is centered in a regu-
lar, although people's, army.

In Guevera's *La Guerra de Guerrillas,* a major theme is
that it is not necessary to wait for fulfillment of all conditions
for a revolution, because the focus of insurrection—that is,
the revolutionary armed bands—can create these conditions.
Here we have no study of cognitive dissonance, no worry about
indicators which point to a revolutionary situation. Qualitative
rather than quantitative judgments about ripeness for revolution are made (Guevara's recent failures will no doubt give com-
fort to those who aim for more statistical precision). Guevara,
more than Debray (who has in his turn been called an imitator
of Guevara's writings), pays attention to urban insurgency,
which can paralyze industrial and commercial life.

Since the Marxist prophecy of worker revolt in the cities
did not become fulfilled and since the failure of the uprisings in Chinese cities in the late 1920's, much less attention
has been paid to city insurrection than to guerrilla war in the
countryside. Even the Budapest and Poznan uprisings and the
earlier Warsaw Ghetto uprising did not reinvigorate interest
in the cities, since cities seemed to provide neither a social
and political base for armed insurrection nor a favorable military field of action. Guevara saw the possibilities of Latin
American cities' aiding guerrilla *focos.* But he did not give
the cities a primary role, and in Debray the Llano receded
even further in importance and emerged really as a hostile
or negative force. It has been riot in American cities which

has led to a reemphasis on revolutionary potential in the cities. Aside from works treating ghetto uprisings in America, the cities remain a focus for work on coups, but not on revolution.

Guerrilla war, unconventional war, counterinsurgency, *guerre révolutionaire,* civic action—these terms have begun to occupy more and more space in writings on developing areas. Many authors have seen a specially close connection between the process of nation-building and the prevalence of insurgency. In a number of writings, Lucien Pye has analyzed this connection. In his work on Burma, Pye saw an acculturation process as threatening the modernizing Burmese's sense of identity. As a general proposition we have it that as people are being changed from traditionals into moderns they are likely to be hypersensitive to the deeply felt sensation of being changed and manipulated by others (Pye 1962, pp. 138–39). This sensitivity to being changed is a source of violence in transitional societies. If there are disjunctive socialization processes between basic socialization and political socialization, it is hard for individuals to find identities and insecurity results; there is a confusion of personal complaints and political causes, of personal authority and national unity. In most transitional societies—that is, societies dislocated by the impact of a world culture—people learn that others have hidden hostile feelings toward them; and feelings of aggression that once were channeled and controlled by traditional patterns tend to be released in diffuse and unpredictable directions (p. 54). Since change produces more insecurity, there must be a quantitative increase in the degree of aggression and hostility within society.

But does all change produce more insecurity? And more

specifically, what are the characteristics of a transitional society? Some individuals have argued circularly about transitional societies. They turn out to be societies in transition without specification of properties that indeed put them into the category. The only criterion which often emerges is the fact of instability. Of course, there have been arguments that particular people have a propensity for violence and that as given societies modernize, violence will decline. Pye reports that many Burmese felt that way about their own society and believed that traditional rather than modernized groups committed violence. The facts did not confirm this to Pye (p. 166), and there was no clear connection between acculturation to the modern world and a decline in violence. Indeed, undergoing the process inclined individuals to violence.

For Pye, the real problem of political development is the extent to which socialization processes of a people provide them with new associational sentiments so that they can have considerable conflict without destroying the stability of the system (p. 52). When such sentiments are lacking, a polity cannot even endure moderate levels of controversy. (How do we know whether such sentiments exist except by deduction?) Pye's theory of modernization is that creating effective, purposeful, adaptive, more complex, and rationalized organizations means being modern and developed (p. 38). But ought we not to recognize that not only pathological individuals but also social groups may thrive politically on the physical elimination of others? Organizations such as Pye has in mind for fulfillment of criteria of modernity may not only be used for violence but may be constructed through violence.

Others besides Pye have stressed the prevalence of violence in new states and transitional societies. We find the view that old antagonisms born of primordial sentiments reappear in new forms and often with new politicized guise, when former ly colonial states become independent. In fact, by virtue of the politicization of ethnic or religious disputes in the new context of the new state, old antagonisms may emerge with greater intensity and scope (Le Vine, p. 71). They may become violent for the first time if they have not been violently expressed heretofore, as participants acquire new perspectives and find more effective ways of expressing antagonisms. We have numerous examples of increased violence, either as central government tries to impose itself over parochial groups (Bienen) or as groups vie with each other for higher stakes or become aware of other groups in new ways (Zolberg 1966*b*; Young, Anderson, and Von der Mehden; Geertz 1963). The view has often been put forward that violence tends to increase as effective control that government can exercise lessens. But violence can increase as government *tries* to establish central control or has a strict (in Pye's terms, administrative) view of its governmental functions.

The lack of political integration in new states has been cited over and over again as a primary cause, indeed a prerequisite, for violence. Social and geographic bases for violence are provided by ethnic, regional, or communal splits. Societie with such "gaps" (as Shils, Geertz, and Pye have described) ar agrarian societies or societies where there are extreme differences between urban and rural patterns of life (Pye 1964, p. 163). Thus it is argued that highly complex industrial societies at one end of the spectrum and homogeneously integrated ones at the other will show infrequent insurgency. In between we have transitional societies—new nations, underdeveloped countries with high rates of political violence. The proposition has been formulated by the Feierabends as follows: The highest and lowest points of the modernity continuum will tend to produce maximum stability in the political order, whereas a medium position on the continuum will produce maximum instability. This proposition embodied the basic properties of the frustration-aggression theory (where the higher the social-want formation in any given society and the lower the social-want satisfaction, the greater the systemic frustration and the greater the impulse to political instability. (Note that instability rather than violence is mentioned here; in the Feierabends' work not all measures of instability involve violence.) The proposition was said to owe debts to a literature on modernization. The idea is that modernization creates new wants as well as leads to their satisfaction in the long run. The peak discrepancy between systemic goals and their frustration should come somewhere in the middle of the transitional phase between traditional society and the achievement of modernity. The frustration index was a ratio of combined coded score on satisfaction indices (GNP, caloric intake, telephones, physicians, newspapers, radios) divided by a country's coded literacy rate or urbanization score. The Feierabends did not get the expected curvilinear lows and highs of instability on their runs. They proposed that early exposure to modernity is a maximum one and no increasing rates of desire for it follow. There was also a problem in finding truly traditional societies.

Highly industrialized societies can show plenty of political violence. To say that these are societies with cleavages is not good enough. The proposition that where there are no cleavages there will be no violence is tautological, if cleavage is derived from the phenomenon of conflict itself. (I am not suggesting that the Feierabends do this.) There can be cleavage in society in the sense of extreme ethnic heterogeneity, rural-urban gaps, and wide differences of incomes between occupational groups without violence obtaining. And violence can take place without cleavage showing in "objective" indices Violence can be legitimate or institutionalized violence, as in pastoral tribal feuds, knighthood jousts, clan feuding. Or to the outside observer, a relatively homogeneous society may be violently torn apart. What is interesting about the proposed connection between violence and so-called transitional societies is not propositions about lack of integration but rather propositions about rates and patterns of change or no change and violence. Will violence come about when there are high rates of change—which can be measured as increased literacy, urbanization, income growth? In terms of growth rates, some developed countries (USSR; recently USA, West Germany, Japan) get higher rates of income growth than most developing countries. The Feierabends suggest that income growth is the one exception to rapid change and instability moving in the same direction. It is likely that structural change in economy will be better indicators, since high growth rates can come about in underdeveloped countries, should prices rise for one major export. Surely, "growth" without structural change is worth focusing on.

Many commentators have pointed to a connection between rates of change, the breaking up of traditional societies, and increased violence. Fewer have noted the relative lack of violence in colonially ruled areas. Why so little violence against colonial rule, or is it that we simply have poor data on the amount of violence? Large-scale, anticolonial, violent uprisings occurred in China, Malaya, Madagascar, Algeria, Arabia,

and Indochina; to lesser extents in Kenya, Indonesia, and
Angola in the twentieth century, but not everywhere in Asia
and Africa. Insofar as there have been attempts to account
for the relative lack of anticolonial violence, answers have
ranged from Mannoni's and Fanon's stress on the acceptance
of inferiority on the part of subject peoples to recognition of
superior force, a force which then becomes vitiated by world
war in Europe and the rise of the non-European great powers,
who became willing to provide weapons and aid to insurgents.
Others have focused on the good government that colonial
powers provided or the absence of enough colonial disruption
of traditional society to create the social disorganization prerequisite to large-scale violence. The corollary here is that,
once society is disorganized, military power becomes one of
the few effective means for achieving political goals (Pye 1956,
p. 28).

Considering treatments of insurgency with a view toward
recommending policies for countering insurgency, we see a
basic division over the roots of insurgency and basic differences over means of confronting it. Theorists of counterinsurgency tell us that unconventional warfare is not new. Ir-
regulars are as old as war, and the linking of violence by small
groups—ambushes, raids, terrorism—to psychological warfare,
which defines all violent and nonviolent measures undertaken
to influence an opponent rather than to annihilate him (which
the French formulate as revolutionary warfare), is not perceived as new either (see Greene, Paret and Shy, Pustay,
Osanka). Paret and Shy, however, argue that the development
of the modern state creates new means and new motives for
conflict. This is not explained at length beyond treating the
connection between domestic insurgents and foreign helpers

or instigators. Is there something unique about contemporary insurrection?

If internal war takes place during periods of transition and in societies that are poorly integrated, we should expect to find it not only in the post-colonial period of the twentieth century but in other post-colonial periods and periods of transition. And, as Eckstein points out, there is a high incidence of internal war in late antiquity, the Renaissance, the Reformation, and the early nineteenth century. There has been a theme in American writing on insurgency that a significant number of rebels can be mobilized only if a people have been grossly mistreated. There is a deep strain in British writing which sees insurgency as springing from man's inherent and compulsively irrational urge to violence and mischief. Not much new is attributed in either view since neither injustice nor man's nature is a peculiarly twentieth-century phenomenon. Nor are the policy conclusions which have followed from the general analyses aimed at dealing with uniquely modern political crises. The "American" conclusion has usually in the past been reform and the British is police work.

Since there has been the perception that "brutality, fear and the resultant social disorganization can only work for the guerrilla, no matter who initiates them" (Paret and Shy, p. 48), the American solution has been a two-pronged attack on the "root causes" of social injustice and the military struggle whose continuation makes impossible stability and the building of responsive political institutions. In the past, the American emphasis was, at least rhetorically, on social reform in order to remove the grievances upon which insurgents fed. Recently, American writing on insurgency has

taken a somewhat different direction. American theorists
have been reading the literature on the great revolution. Conscious of the proposition that social change brought about by
attempts at reform may weaken governments' positions, they
either argue for a slowing up of social mobilization (Huntington
1966) so that institutionalization can take place, or they argue
that, since even if reform programs influence popular support
for government there "may be no effect or a perverse effect,
on the cost and availability of inputs that the insurgents require for their operations" (Wolfe), rural improvement programs must attempt to exact something in return for whatever benefits are provided. That is, for counterinsurgency to
work, not improvement programs pure and simple, but *quid
pro quo* programs are necessary in rural areas where government is being challenged (pp. 52-54). The objective of popular support for government, which was once thought to be
sufficient to separate the guerrilla-fish from the people-sea,
is now seen as being too broad because it cannot discrimi-
nate between government actions that hinder and government actions that help insurgent operations. Moreover, it is
too ambitious for an overburdened government. Government
cannot overcome in short order the attitudes in societies where
government has always been viewed as opponent rather than
friend. To develop modern societies it is necessary to change
these attitudes, but this is a long-run effort—twenty-five
years is probably too short a horizon. Increasing popularity
will be a consequence of successful counterinsurgency rather
than a cause of it. The alternative that Wolfe proposes is to
deprive insurgents of inputs. It is necessary to raise the cost
and reduce the availability of inputs and to curtail the outputs of the system that the insurgents constitute, by

interfering with the process by which inputs are converted to outputs and by directly curtailing the system's outputs (p. 56 This may sound like a lead up to counterterror and to emphasis solely on military techniques against insurgency. However, it is aimed primarily at forming policies for nonmilitary input-oriented measures. For example, policies that would increase rural income by raising food prices or projects that would increase agricultural productivity through distribution of fertilizer or livestock are seen by Wolfe as possibly being negative in value during an insurgency. It is necessary to understand in detail how the organization of insurgents functions in specific contexts. Pye says this can best be done by distinguishing the goals, methods or recruitment, and indoctrination of the insurgents as well as organizational characteristics and the propensities in decision-making and actions (1964, pp. 164-66), and he himself undertook such a study of the insurgent movement in Malaya, where he saw rootless individuals who believed that hostility and aggressiveness were characteristic of political activities and that physical violence was likely to be the final arbiter in politics (1956, p. 168). In a tactics-dominated organization such as existed in Malaya, it was hard to shift from violence to peaceful revolutionary activity, and thus the insurgents became prisoners of terrorism which became counterproductive. The insurgents were people fascinated with means but with little way of appraising ends (p. 345). The unambiguous character of violence was important to them, but their impatience and commitment to violence led to tactical inflexibility. But Pye more than Wolfe, also concerns himself with the character of the government against which the insurrection is aimed (1964, p. 165), and with the organization of the general society in which the insurrection occurs, taking heed of Aristotle's maxim that the character of revolution and violence depends on the polity in which it takes place. Wolfe lists a number of measures to be taken to influence insurgent behaviors, rather than attitudes, by raising costs of inputs to the insurgency movement: e.g., buy up rural food supplies to cut off flows to guerrillas; give money for insurgent capture or for information; disrupt logistics via logistical means; tighten military discipline among counterinsurgents; connect social-improvement programs with the kind of population behavior government wants, via incentives for that behavior; provide military protection for rural people; and initiate civic-action projects by the military which expand instruments available to government for obtaining information and controlling insurgent logistics (pp. 59-69).

Of course, if government could carry out programs such as purchase of rural foodstuffs and civic action without corruption and further antagonizing of the population, insurgency *might* not have started. It may be no easier for government to act as "good" government in the Wolfe projects than in social-reform programs in general. It is possible that insurgency starts by a small group that does not have mass support to begin with but builds such support. Guerrillas then take a calculated risk—given that the sea may easily run dry—that their support is fragile. The whole conception of incentives for rural population to turn in guerrillas is based on the premise of fragile support—that rural behaviors can be influenced in this way. The Philippines and Kenya are cited as examples where it worked. But where indeed is the chicken and the egg? Both movements were highly restricted to begin with. As a tactic of counterinsurgency Wolfe's program has a hope of success only where discontent is ethnically circumscribed or otherwise not generalized throughout society, and the guerrillas are met early in the game. In Vietnam it has proved ineffective. But even for the start of insurrection, cannot the argument be made that this is a program wherein the proponents are fascinated with means but have little way of appraising ends? For ends have to do with the nature of society, which can be expressed here as relationships between insurgents and society and between government and society as well as between government and insurgents. The capacity of a political and social organism to defend itself depends on elite will and effectiveness, which in turn depend at least in part on the elite's sense of its own legitimacy, not only on its ability to choose correct tactics, although these may strengthen the will and confidence of elites.

Another and perhaps more basic matter: What is America's interest in defeating insurgents? If insurgents are communist-inspired, this might or might not be seen as a threat to American interests, depending on one's view of insurgent potential alliances—and international politics in general. Are there basic American concerns with the nature of societies themselves? This is stated to be so, in terms of democracy, self-determination, freedom, etc. In that case, is it transformations of society rather than insurgent defeat solely that ought to occupy us? This also applies to the slow-up modernization argument, which presumes that weak governments can slow up social mobilization. And if a major interest is in peaceful change, both because that is an end unto itself and because violent change may create international problems of involvement of great powers, then is there perhaps an American stake in choosing probable winners, even if they are insurgents against regimes allied to the USA? Again, if the best tactic in guerrilla warfare is preventing the insurrection, assuming that the next-best tactic is meeting insurrection early rather than late (unless one has a "Let a hundred flowers bloom" tactic), then are, perhaps, radical transformation programs rather than social reform programs appropriate?

The American government's most recent position has been the Wolfe one, although Wolfe would disagree over the content of AID programs. Numerous present and past officials have argued: "Communist guerrillas are gaining for the very simple reason known as guns, bombs, fighters" (Walt Rostow addressing the Army Special Warfare School at Fort Bragg, in Paret and Shy, p. 62). Rostow does not deny that some kind of revolutionary process is going on in the world. But he focuses on the communist attempt to exploit it—the communists are the scavengers of the transition. Yet everything we know of the conditions of fighting as guerrilla against government gives evidence of the hardships involved, the physical and psychological strains sustained by strong commitments which often grow stronger under these pressures. Paret and Shy say that "terror, which guerrillas may or may not employ as a primary weapon, has received less systematic analysis than any other component of irregular warfare." Perhaps this is finally a case in the social sciences, where absence of treatment is some reflection of relative importance in analyzing factors in a social process. This is not to say that violence is not a crucial subject for analysis, but only that terror as a weapon of guerrillas may not be the most interesting or important phenomenon of insurrection.

Paret and Shy argue that "comprehensive change—call it

modernization or Westernization—is a process that current-
ly makes most of the world vulnerable to internal warfare; to
speed and control this process is in the American interest."
They recognize that warfare may be initiated despite, or even
because of, attempts at getting fundamental change (p. 79).
Nonetheless, it is up to government to correctly analyze social groups so that specific reforms can drain off insurgent
sources of strength. The focus is on governments' abilities to
make major political adjustments and allocate nonmilitary re-
sources in a militarily remunerative way. The long-term task
is modernization.

Guerrillas emerge in a basic division as symptoms or causes
as when opinion divides over whether riots in Cambridge,
Maryland, stem from speeches by Rap Brown or not. In the
writings of present and former officials of the U.S. government on guerrilla war, it is often stressed that the existence
of guerrillas is not positive proof that government is unpop-
ular. And although in the long run economic development,
modernization, and reform are seen as key factors in creating popular support and stable government; it is argued that
guerrillas can thrive as modernization, economic reform, and
economic development go forward (Hilsman, p. 30). A crucial part of this argument is to see the mass of the country as
being apathetic, rather than committed to government or to
insurrectionists. There are not so many pro-and-con commitments, because government's presence is rare. A small
minority is both pro- and antigovernment. The aim of
counterinsurgency is to give no quarter to the insurrectionists but, at the same time, not to antagonize the mass.

The notion of an apathetic mass which remains on the
sidelines is not a theme only of American writers on coun-

terinsurgency. It comes into a great body of writing by revolutionaries in a number of ways and with various degrees of force and explicitness. Lenin's arguments with the Mensheviks over the role of Social Democratic organization involved a fundamental disagreement about the way social democratic consciousness would come about. Lenin believed that a working-class movement could not naturally grow to political consciousness and organization and that it could do so only under the active leadership of a Social Democratic party. Yet he did see a "spontaneous" revolutionary workers' movement. The need was to direct this movement to create true revolutionary consciousness (Haimson 1955). I have already noted that Lenin envisioned the furtherance of class solidarity by a directed use of violence where the solidarity of the vanguard with the proletariat would be both achieved and expressed through violence. Debray's and Guevara's insistence that armed bands create the conditions for a revolution goes even farther. Both share Lenin's suspicion of the peasantry—a suspicion somewhat hidden in Debray by his posing of Sierra and Llano. But note that "Sierra" is not a synonym for peasantry.

The recent failures of the Guevara-inspired insurgency in Bolivia may confirm some revolutionaries in their suspicions of peasant revolutionary fervor. But this failure also seems to confirm the need for a peasant ocean for insurgent fish to swim in. One Harry Villegas, a Cuban who operated with Guevara in Bolivia, was asked, on arrival in Chile, why the guerrillas were unable to gain the support of Bolivia's peasants. He was quoted as replying: "Because peasants are always with forces of power and strength. We did not reach the necessary phase of power. A guerrilla movement has three steps. The first is forming a people's army against the government. Next the guerrilla army becomes as powerful as the army. Finally, the guerrillas become the power in the coun try. That is when the peasants support them. We lost our fight before reaching the second step" (*New York Times,* February 24, 1968). But this argument, which many American writers on insurgency would be very comfortable with, implies that th second and third steps can be reached without peasant suppor

Quite a different position is stated by Johnson (1962*b*), who argued that civilian loyalties are crucial for guerrillas. He stressed the mass base of the guerrillas and insisted that there are no instances of guerrilla success with terrorism alone. The mobilizing influence on the masses is the hated condition. But in both arguments modernization is seen as essential in the lor haul but of not much use in the short run. Modernization here really means generalized change; it does not have specific con tent. Modernization is seen as uprooting the established so cial system, producing political and economic dislocation and tension. Johnson sees a long-term process for changing the abi ities of local elites, class structure, and the economy. Thus neg tiated stalemate may be necessary. Again, prevention is the be ter part of cure; antiguerrilla terrorism is likely to facilitate th mass mobilization on which the guerrillas thrive. Yet it is reco nized that there is mounting unrest worldwide in rural areas; peasants want social justice and reform at a minimum. They also crave physical security and peace. Thus some program of social reform is needed too (Hilsman, p. 32). It is necessary to indicate that the path to modernization is being taken. It is rather clear that in this analysis the implicit meaning of modernization is not generalized social change but rather change in a direction—to development in the sense of eco nomic growth and physical security.

Social mobility is one aspect of modernization that seems relatively neglected in much of the current writing on counterinsurgency. This is perhaps surprising, since concern with social mobility has a rather long pedigree which can be traced through the writings of revolutionaries. There simply has not been enough attention paid to peasants who no longer want to be peasants or who want to fundamentally alter the status relationships between themselves and other peasants or themselves and nonpeasants. Schurmann's work on China stressed social mobility, whereas Johnson (1962*a*) emphasized peasant nationalism as a primary factor in gaining peasant support for revolution. (McAlister's soon-to-be-published work on Vietnam focuses on social mobility in the Vietnamese Revolution.)

In much of the literature on counterinsurgency it can be said that one conception of modernization is not used—that modernization means, at a minimum, a social system that can constantly innovate without falling apart, including innovations in beliefs about the acceptability of change (Apter 1965, p. 62); or, in Halpern's terms, that modernization demands of all systems of society the capacity which the scientific community already possesses: the ability to persist continuously in the enterprise of responding to the challenge of new questions, new facts, . . . by developing, maintaining, modifying, and disintegrating systems of theory—by creating systems that derive their stability from their intrinsic capacity to generate and absorb continuing transformation (pp. 173 n., 175). I think there is good reason why such conceptions of modernization have not been much used when so much else of the language and even the spirit and thought of writing on modernization have. The policymaker asks: Transform what concrete structures in society? Innovate where? How do you constantly innovate without falling apart, and what is falling apart—real countries or analytic systems? What does persistent transformation mean? In the absence of answers to such questions it is perhaps not too surprising that emphasis is on training armed forces to be counterinsurgency forces, on civic-action programs, and on building local police forces that can handle the unrest exported to the cities as urbanization proceeds (an argument which crops up in America as a call for the "new" type of policeman). Much more congenial to policymakers confronted with devising programs for counterinsurgency has been a conception of modernity which stresses that power moves toward those who command the tools of modern technology, especially modern weapons (Rostow). Interesting is the different place of science in the two conceptions of modernization. Apter (1965, p. 62) sees modernization as a special framework that can provide skills and knowledge necessary for living in a technologically advanced world, including the ability to communicate in terms of technology. And Halpern sees the scientific community as already possessing the capacity of a modern system—the ability to constantly innovate. For Rostow, the introduction of modern technology is the key to modernization (p. 55).

We also find in Rostow a view that once the transitional stage is passed through incumbents will be all right. Part of this reasoning depends on a view of the transition we have already touched on—identity problems and government's vulnerability in societies where old patterns are disrupted and new ones not established yet. And passing through the transition means to Rostow the solving of problems inherited from traditional society. In this argument, however, there is also the view that once modern technology is spread in the society the game is won, because the aim of development is the adoption of modern technology. Moreover, implicit here is the idea that modern technology can defeat insurrectionists. But, as many people have pointed out, the stages are not such historically (or heuristically) neat devices. Violence takes place in technologically advanced societies. The problems of society are not solved in any stage. It is an open question whether economically advanced societies will be violence-free as solutions to problems are grappled with or not.

Thus, seeing modernization as an end state or as a process of constant innovation influences views about the prospects for violent politics, and views of what to do about violence depend on conceptions of modernization.

3. REVOLUTION

> *"But where can we draw water,"*
> *Said Pearse to Connolly,*
> *"When all the wells are parched away?*
> *O plain as plain can be*
> *There's nothing but our own red blood*
> *Can make a right Rose Tree."*
>
> William Butler Yeats

Innumerable writers have pointed out that revolution is a vague and equivocal term. Its use hinges sometimes on the presence of violence and judgment about discontinuity (Gerschenkron 1964, p. 180). Most contemporary writers on revolution share with Chalmers Johnson (1967) the view that revolutionary change is a special kind of change, "one that involves the intrusion of violence into civil social relations." Some, like Johnson, set out to examine the meaning of social change. None seem to have generalized about the effects of violence on change. In fact, once revolution is defined in terms of violence, emphasis shifts to explaining the kinds of change involved in revolution, sometimes in a circular way, but the place of violence per se seems neglected. Johnson (pp. 7-10) asks: Sociologically speaking, what do we mean by violence? He then *defines* violence either as behavior which is impossible for others to orient themselves to or as behavior which is deliberately intended to prevent orientation and the development of stable expectations with regard to it. Thus violence emerges as a contingent concept dependent on the prior existence of a system of social action within which it takes place. Revolution, too, is a contingent concern; it is one form of violence (p. 11). "True revolution . . . is the acceptance of violence in order to cause the system to change when all else has failed, and the very idea of revolution is contingent upon this perception of societal failure" (p.12). This seems to me either tautological or false, depending on the use of the word "true." There is another problem in defining violence as behavior which is impossible for others to orient themselves to or behavior which is deliberately intended to prevent orientation and development of stable expectations with regard to it. What of those who use violence with the expectation that the targets will surrender? Surely at least some use of violence is predicated on others forming stable expectations with regard to it. No possible instrumental use of violence could come under Johnson's understanding of violence.

Johnson has explicit concern for violence and change, and his contingent concepts seem representative of much of the writing on revolution which utilizes, implicitly or explicitly, social-systems analysis. There is no quarrel with analyzing political violence within a social context. Where else would one analyze it? Johnson believes that "any analytical penetration of the behavior characterized as 'purposive political violence' must utilize as its prime tool a conception of the social context in which it occurs" (p. 14). I am suggesting that there is a problem in defining violence in terms of a conception of a social system, then defining *the* system (a revolutionary one) in terms of a concept of violence. It is all true by definition, but so what? What concrete changes are taking place through violence which, in a simple-minded way, we can measure rather easily?

I might mention two more problems I found in reading Johnson which seem to come up frequently. Johnson makes the statement—with reference to revolution not yet occurring in America—"The fact that a revolution has not yet occurred illustrates the principle that socialized actors will resort to violence only when all other means have been blocked" (p. 96). This is an assertion about violence as a last resort. As a statement about violence it was false when written. Violence has been used by whites and Negroes frequently. For the statement—revolution will occur when means of peaceful change have been blocked—to be meaningful, mechanisms of peaceful political change have to be shown and their blockage shown too, concretely. And specific changes meant by revolution have to be drawn. Otherwise one can always argue as follows, and nothing can constitute disproof: No revolution—well, it's because all other means have not been blocked

The third problem: There has emerged consensus around the view that socioeconomic change lies behind any revolution. This view has been expressed in many ways: when things get better, but expectations nonetheless snowball, then revolutions occur (rising expectations); or more generally, when society's values and the realities with which it must deal in order to exist are in harmony with each other, the society is immune from revolution. (For a discussion of theories of homeostatic equilibrium, see Johnson [1967, pp. 59-87].) Another version of the last is the theory of "correlated moderates," which in Feldman's words (pp. 113-14) ". . . assumes that societies are in stasis *only* when different rates of change—political, economic, and social—enjoy some kind of equivalence at a moderate level." This theory is analogous to a certain economic development theory, which sees change as necessary everywhere and at once. Similarly, in these theories all the subsystems must change at once or somehow be in harmony. Revolutions are those sporadic periods when they are not. Feldman's complaint with these ideas is that such assumptions and conceptions lead to an inability to deal meaningfully with sources of discordance and disequilibration that are ever-present in social systems. My problem is that the disequilibria referred to are in analytical systems. How does one measure disequilibria by comparing analytical systems? What is out of whack with what? Now, in fact, relations turn out to be drawn between, e.g., unemployment rates or lack of redress in the legal system and receptivity to ideologies. But now people think they are talking about something other than analytical subsystems. In other words, the models are abandoned. What is out of whack is never clear. Why imbalance is important for violence and change remains a mystery to me unless one believes that somehow violence comes about when analytical subsystems are disequilibrated, which seems to involve either reification or argument by strange analogy.

Thus in the literature on revolution, where there is an attempt to treat violence and change, most of the effort is in definitions, which after all is not a useless endeavor by any means. But most analysts make rather different claims, purporting to show actual relationships. Yet rarely are violence and some specified change or changes treated as variables in dependent and independent relationships. In the literature on insurgency, guerrilla war, and counterinsurgency, there is more specification of the relationship of violence and change and much more concern with typologies of violence, measurement of violence, and duration of violence. But there is often little sense of what change means. I do not want to review the etymology of revolution; among others, Johnson does this. I do wish to briefly examine the concern with the need for violence in transformation.

Mao has said that the central task and the highest form of revolution is to seize political power by armed force and decide issues by war. And he has asserted that "this Marxist-Leninist principle of revolution holds good universally" (Mao *Problems of War and Strategy*, p. 1). Yet Mao has recognized that forms of struggle could be bloodless, that is, nonmilitary in capitalist countries where a legal struggle could be waged. However, when the bourgeoisie was weakened the proletariat would then take up arms and wage war. In Marx, violence and political revolution are linked, but political revolutions mark the transition from one economic system to another. The political event has been preceded by a long-term and fundamental process of change. The political revolution does not create change but is an expression of economic changes. Nevertheless, Marx and Engels saw a real role for physical force and political power. The bourgeois state wields force, and by violence it will be replaced. The proletariat must resort to force. ". . . Force, however, plays another role in history, a revolutionary role; that, in the words of Marx, it is the midwife of every old society which is pregnant with the new, that it is the instrument by the aid of which social movement forces its way through and shatters the dead, fossilised, political forms . . ." (Engels, *Anti-Dühring*, p. 275)

Perhaps more interesting than the causal or definitional connections between violence and change (for our purposes is the role of violence in the creating of something new, which is implied in the quote above. As Lenin noted, in *State and Revolution* (1932, p. 19), Engels provides a veritable panegyric on violent revolution. Engels speaks of the immense spiritual and moral regeneration which has resulted from every victorious revolution. National consciousness in

Germany had been permeated by servility as a result of the
Thirty Years' War, and a violent revolution could wipe it out.
Herr Dühring had believed that the use of force demoralized
the person who used it. For Lenin, the correct and organized
use of force would bring about the strengthening of class consciousness. Yet there is no glorification of violence in Lenin.
Above all, Lenin was against the spontaneous use of violence
and thus turned against a strain in the Russian revolutionary
movement which had stressed either spontaneous violence
by the masses or individual acts of terrorism. There were also individuals in Russian Populism who had stressed the use
of disciplined, professional terrorism (e.g., Nechaev and
Tkachev). One accusation that was leveled against Lenin from
within Russian (and German) social democracy was that he
was teaching the masses to destroy the old order before they
fully grasped the meaning of their actions. Those who were
against conspiratorial politics made just this argument. They
raised questions about the nature of the new order after destruction. Some anticipated Thermidor. Some Menshevik attacks on Lenin were thus leveled at his espousal of the use of
violence, which they felt was an indication of the unripe conditions and the lack of development of consciousness in the
working class. Reliance on violence was historically self-defeating in the eyes of Menshevik thinkers. Through violence
one despotism could replace another.

Lenin emphasized the creative aspects of political action,
including violent action. Political intervention in the affairs of
society was not trivial. (Wolin states that by mid-nineteenth
century political intervention was seen by socialists as trivial,
not dangerous as St. Simon had believed. For Proudhon, the
task allotted to the nineteenth-century revolution was to

reverse and destroy the political tendencies nourished by 1789 without touching society itself; that is, an attack on government, not society, was called for [Wolin, p. 415].) As the Populists would arrest Russian capitalism by cutting it off forcibly, Lenin would avoid a lengthy bourgeois stage by force.

Sorel maintained that spontaneous action by the masses would be dependent on objective material conditions but would be violent and lead to change. For Sorel, only economic action would be truly revolutionary; revolutionary action would be in the form of a general strike. Sorel argued that the proletariat finds in its conditions of life something to nourish sentiments of solidarity and revolt; it is in daily warfare with hierarchy and property; it can thus conceive moral values opposed to those consecrated by tradition. In other words, through struggle, the proletariat is a force for a new and healthy society, whereas the middle classes cannot find in their conditions of life any source which stands in opposition to bourgeois ideas; the notion of catastrophe escapes them entirely (see Carr on Sorel). For Sorel, not only was the proletariat the carrier of a new moral force, but through its actions it would purify Europe. Sorel said little about the society which would follow proletariat victory. Of interest to us is Sorel's faith in regenerated human nature—regenerated through violence.

As we have already noted, this idea was sounded by Fanon and it was, of course, evident in both Fascist and Nazi doctrines. For Fanon, a true new beginning was needed. This was to be achieved through national revolution. The colonized must struggle for political freedom in order to achieve personal freedom. Violence would have a purifying flame. Participation in revolution would have therapeutic effects on man and society. Colonized masses would become transfigured through combat, as they would through Sorel's general strike (see Zolberg [1964] on Fanon). Total praxis would be brought by combat. But Fanon was not merely claiming that individuals and society would be somehow transfigured through struggle. He pointed to specific structural changes taking place in Algeria during the revolution. The family was undergoing a mutation; revolutionary attitudes toward technology were taking place as individuals used modern weapons; revolution was shattering the traditional life, and a nation was being forged and prepared for the post-revolutionary period, a nation consecrated in blood.

For Fanon, true decolonization was the replacing of one species of man by another. (This theme of the new man was also found throughout the Russian revolutionary tradition.) Colonialism had been imposed through violence and had at first provoked a reaction of violence turning inward, an argument now also current in America to explain Negro violence. Fanon saw increased muscular tension in colonized individuals and heightened criminality within the community. In ternally directed violence must be redirected to external objects. Not only would this bring personal freedom but society's transformation as well. The most powerful reservoir of violence was the peasantry. It alone was revolutionary, as cities were themselves artificial creations of colonialism. The peasants would sweep everything before them without compromise. But the violent potential of the people must be channeled by the vanguard or it could spend itself uselessly. As Zolberg points out, Fanon believed that armed struggle might be symbolic sometimes; it was the commitment to violence rather than the consummation of violent acts which was stressed. Through this commitment to violence, the evil of violence would be exorcised. Fanon believed that violence would be cleansing, but it would be a cleansing pathology.

It may be useful here to introduce a political thinker concerned with the economy of violence and one acclaimed by many as the first truly modern political thinker, Machiavelli. Machiavelli accounted for a rise in violence as legitimacy broke down. He "sensed correctly that in recent centuries the rapid changes in institutional forms, social structures, and types of leadership had rendered old notions of legitimacy obsolete" (Wolin, p. 200). Machiavelli was also concerned with instruments and forms of violence. He perceived that the arts of violence were crucial for taking and consolidating power in an already unstable situation. And he focused on problems of mobility which were to be raised so provocatively again by Mosca and Pareto. Wolin has said that Machiavelli aimed at the political arriviste, the figure who bedevils modern politics. The man of humble origin who rose to be prince was the offspring of an age of restless ambition and rapid transformations, an age which saw quick shifts in power among elite groups. In this context, Machiavelli saw the challenge of reducing the scope of violence. Machiavelli tells us that, in a corrupt age, greatness can be attained only by immoral means. For Machiavelli, violence could be legitimate because crimes committed by political actors fell under the judgments of history, not morality; whereas for Augustine, violence was an original sin (Wolin, p. 209). (As for Harrington: "No man shall show me a commonwealth born crooked that ever became straight.") It was national greatness which legitimated violence, according to Machiavelli.

For Machiavelli, the role of the political actor—he who acts in limited political space—was to dispense violence. This was most sharply defined for the ruler who, after seizing power, was compelled to "organize everything in that state afresh. ... The new prince, above all other princes, cannot possibly avoid the name of cruel." Machiavelli took up the problem of the cumulative effect in society of the consistent application of coercion and the not infrequent use of violence. The task of a science of politics was a controlled application of force (Wolin, p. 221). The line between political creativity and destruction could be maintained only by a precise dosage of violence which was appropriate to specific situations. While this line was especially fine in periods of flux, it was one always to be drawn. Here Machiavelli was different from classical and medieval theorists and from most contemporary theorists of guerrilla war. In classical and medieval theory, once affairs are set in motion along proper paths—spread of knowledge, proper education, improvement of social morality—then the pressures from an ordered environment would begin to operate and there would be less need for a systematic application of force (Wolin, p. 220). In our own time we have the view that once economic development is achieved, or the transition period is passed, or political institutionalization takes place, a lessening of violence and the need for violence occurs. Violence, then, is attributed to a failure to solve problems which arise under a number of objectively specifiable conditions. Machiavelli envisioned the possibility of reducing violence, but he stressed the acts of creative leadership which would be necessary. He noted the importance of law, political institutions, and habits of civility that in regularizing human behavior helped to reduce the number of instances in which force and fear had to be applied. Popular consent represented a form of social power which, if properly exploited, reduced the amount of violence directed at society as a whole. Indeed, in corrupt societies, violence represented the only means of arresting decadence and restoring civic consciousness to the citizens. But above all, the focus is on elites here. There are no vague and romantic ideas about purifying violence; rather the emphasis is on the costs of violence, the need for violence, and the mechanisms, habits of mind, and concerns which can minimize costs. At the same time, Machiavelli was not for minimizing violence at the expense of social change. He did not believe this possible in any case. He spoke to the problem of how to control change, constantly innovate, and use violence judiciously.

Machiavelli, unlike many contemporary social theorists, did not see violence as something pathological in the sense that it was temporary, infrequent, and unnatural in society. Stable order has been used interchangeably with natural order, and systems theories which use equilibrium as a core concept see societies moving toward or away from equilibrium, a natural state. Since large-scale violence is often correlated with profound social change, far-reaching change, too, can be seen as pathological (Feldman points this out). A number of contributors to the Eckstein volume *Internal War* have noted that contemporary social theory has little to say about the occurrence of large-scale violence, since violence is conceived of as being incidental to the basic character of social structures and processes as a stable image of social life is projected (Feldman, pp. 111-12). (Violence is seen as an incidental phenomenon, but not a pathological one, in much of the Marxist literature as well, but not in Sorel or Fanon or Machiavelli.)

Revolution has been conceived usually as political and
social changes which proceed rapidly and with violence and
which have extremely far-reaching consequences (Dahrendorf).
Revolution is change effected by use of violence in government, regime, and society (Johnson 1967). Arendt, however,
sees revolution tied to a conception of changing the course
of history, of beginning anew, which in turn is related to an
idea of freedom. (Barrington Moore [1954] also relates violence to freedom, seeing it as a necessary step to liberty, democracy, and economic progress.) For Arendt (1963, pp.
20-28), violence no more adequately describes the phenomenon of revolution than does change, except where change
is in the sense of a new beginning and where violence is used
to constitute an altogether new body politic. (Arendt argues
that Machiavelli was concerned with renovation, with the
first meaning of revolution, a revolving back to some pre-
established point.) For Arendt, revolution, properly speaking, did not exist before the modern period. Revolution as
irresistible new beginning she traces to Liancourt's reply to
the King on hearing that the Bastille had fallen. When Louis
said, "C'est une révolte," Liancourt replied, "Non, Sire, c'est
une Révolution." The meaning here is twofold: something
irresistible was occurring; and the people had directly entered.
Revolution opened the door to household cares, or, as others
might say, economic and social needs (p. 86). And only violence is strong and swift enough to help people directly when
personal problems are at stake. For Arendt, violence can be
used to destroy power, as when order is ended; but violence
also is necessary for new beginnings (p. 149). This is so because, in Arendt's language (following Harrington), violence

is the instrument of direct intervention in politics, and because to fabricate means to create something "not out of nothing but out of a given material which must be violated to yield itself to the formative process out of which a thing, a fabricated object, will arise" (pp. 209-10). But though violence seems necessary to Arendt, at least for new beginnings, under the conditions of most polities (but not of eighteenth-century America) the revolutionaries' hope that violence will conquer poverty is to no avail. "La terreur as a means to achieve le bonheur sent revolutions and revolutionaries to their doom" (p. 224). Arendt, too, believes in original sin. More than this, for Arendt, violence is marginal to the political realm. Where there is violence, speech ends. Arendt concludes that political theory has little to say about violence and waives its discussion to technicians because of the speechlessness involved. A theory of revolution can deal only with the justification for violence.

If the justification of violence is social change, or progress, or modernization, then three propositions must be confronted (1) Most social and political change does not result from violent revolution. (2) Where violent revolutions have occurred they constitute much more of a watershed in a slower process than an immediate and radical reordering of society. Moreover, watersheds can be found in nonrevolutionary societies too (Bendix). (3) Large-scale violence can be associated with "the more things change, the more they remain the same," as Mosca pointed out with reference to violence in the Italian communes and the Greek states. Mosca also argued that progress—the rise of Hellenic art and society, emancipation of serfs, and rebirth of letters at the end of the Middle Ages—developed independently of bloody strug-

gles of the times, and, at most, civil conflicts helped to re-
tard the maturing of such movements. They functioned in
this respect like pestilence, famine, or foreign wars (Mosca,
p. 202). Mosca further stressed that fundamental changes in
society can be made with the consent or on the initiative of
the ruling class.

Stone (1967) argues against the view of Moore (1966)
that violence, and in particular the violent destruction of the
peasantry, is a necessary prerequisite of a democratic society.
He points out that in England the process was very slow and
largely free from violence and that in France violence was
used not to transform the peasantry but to reinforce it, and
thus democracy and an independent peasantry have been com-
patible. Stone sees violence as self-defeating because "the
very use of violence creates a new situation demanding a new
solution. (You may have to run faster to stay where you are
in violent politics.) Violence leads to bitter cleavages within
the society which, as the French, English, and American examples suggest, it may take between seventy and 150 years
to weld together. The cost of these cleavages in holding
back the society and preventing its purposeful economic
and political development often outweighs any temporary
gain from the rapid elimination from power of a backward
looking group" (Stone 1967, p. 34).

Stone contends that the evil of great revolutions comes
out of violence in them and that the scale on which violence
is employed in revolutions is determined largely by the personality of the leading actors rather than by the logic of
events. Stone reserves a functional use of bloodletting for
dealing with the relatively rare cases of wholly intransigent
elites who repulse all attempts to modernize or reform.

The great benefit we get from historians concerned with violence and change is their willingness to define change in historical circumstances. Those like Stone and Gerschenkron who then try to generalize provide us with much that is useful. Gerschenkron has suggested that the processes of modern industrialization are the richer and more complex the higher the degree of backwardness on the eve of its great spurt of industrialization. He argues by analogy that the more backward a country the more likely it is that a political revolution will carry out or at least attempt to carry out a larger program of economic measures. If the obstructions are removed from the path of economic progress, the policies are costly and their fruits ripen slowly. "It is not only that, in trying to forestall the revolution in the long run one increases its danger in the short run. In order to carry out positive policies of this type, certain negative measures, most desirable in themsleves, must be postponed" (Gerschenkron 1964, pp. 196-98). Gerschenkron (1962) also suggests that the more backward the country the greater the part played by special institutional factors designed to increase the supply of capital to nascent industry, and the more pronounced the coercion and comprehensiveness of those factors. Implicitly, more violence should be required as well.

Once change is defined, criteria established for recognizing changed situations, and the particular context described, general propositions can be confronted, and one might know whether or not one can count heads in order to begin breaking them or break heads in order to count them (Stone 1966 For Lenin, one could not make an omelet without breaking eggs. But how and where is violence instrumental to change? What about violence that halts or deflects change? There

are many examples of stability imposed by moderate violence only to lead to extreme violence in a longer run; e.g.,
Mexico after Diaz (Huntington 1962, p. 39). Governments
may appear stable as long as their repressive techniques
work; then the deluge (Kling, Russet). Moreover, stable
government (not to say regime) and violence may go together; witness the chronic violence in Colombia.

There are many examples of violence which widen rifts
in societies; where rebels cannot reallocate political power
but where social disorganization results; where violence begets more violence and the predominant motive is personal
and clan vengeance; or where violence is a necessary adjunct
of politics—that is, the politics of how to stay in power
(Dudley, pp. 21-23). Now, depending on the time horizon,
one can see violence leading to change and subsequent re-
consolidation of someone's power. But persistent violence
is also inimical to constant change. For the very fact of persistence of violence means that something indeed is not
changing—the violent situation. Patterns of coup and countercoup fall into the same category of frequent change at a
certain level, but the persistence of a pattern inimical to
change at other levels. There is ample evidence of the situation where leaders of violent movements have no clear idea
of changes to be wrought and where no indication is given
of intent to exercise political authority roles in a fashion different from that heretofore (Young, Anderson, and Von der
Mehden). Have the tasks of modernization been made easier
in the Congo and Nigeria? When we ask: "What social transformations have been wrought by violence?" we should note
that "quantitatively speaking and keeping in mind such aspects of objective social pictures as population, degree of

poverty, ignorance and superstition, who can be sure that, *mutatis mutandis,* the French and Mexican Revolutions were less violent than the Russian and Chinese?" (Sathyamurthy, p. 27).

The other side of the coin is to ask how much change is wrought by nonviolence both in the sense of conscious use of nonviolent doctrines, which have been rather rare, and in the more general sense of change without violence. (See Sathyamurthy [p. 29] on Gandhi's use of nonviolence, where he argues that nonviolence was also marked by concomitant commitment to Ram Raiya, the utopia of traditional community.) In other words, it is necessary for those who see social change as discontinuous and resulting from violence, or associated with violence; those who see social change as a continuous process and ever-present without violence; and those who see violence bringing about political change which ratifies a long process of change to be very precise with regard to the changes that are talked about. What is meant by "system transformation" must be spelled out in detail so that change can be broken up in terms of end results and processes.

The literature on violence has not been noteworthy for attempts to classify change and to relate violence to social processes which are spelled out in detail, although a number of the studies on conflict have tried to do this (Coser, Dahrendorf, Smelser) by explaining structural change in terms of group conflict. And within this literature there are indeed propositions which are neither trivial nor tautological. Dahrendorf, for example, in his study of "structurally generated systematic social conflicts" looks at two variable aspects of social conflict, its intensity and violence. The intensity indicates the degree of involvement of the conflicting parties (p. 211), and the violence indicates the parties' choice of weapons. Dahrendorf gives a number of propositions which relate violence and change:

1) The intensity and violence increase when the political conditions for the organization of conflict groups are absent [p. 213].

2) The intensity and violence increase in proportion to the degree of superimposition of conflicts, either regarding the distribution of authority positions, or the distribution of status positions [p. 239].

3) The intensity increases as social mobility decreases [p. 233].

4) The violence increases when the exclusion from authority positions is accompanied by absolute deprivation in social and economic terms; the intensity increases when the exclusion from authority positions is accompanied by relative deprivation in terms of social and economic status [Kroes].

(Proposition 1 is true by definition unless "the political conditions" are spelled out.)

Rob Kroes applied Dahrendorf's model to a study of the Hungarian revolution and found support for all but the fourth proposition; he concluded that relative, rather than absolute, deprivation must be spoken of in this instance (Kroes, p. 34; I have also used Kroes's outline of Dahrendorf). The kind of testing of models that Kroes did—he looked at Dahrendorf's, Arendt's, Baschwitz's, Davis', Almond's and Gottschalk's models—against the Hungarian revolution seems very promising. There has been little of it done.

There have been, however, increasing efforts at classifying types of violence and creating typologies of violence. This has involved delimitation of forms of violence (Mosca; Eckstein 1964; Leys; Young, Anderson, and Von der Mehden Huntington 1962) where attempts are made to define civil war, coups, revolutions, etc., or to find generic meanings for internal war. Typologies of violence have also been created by looking at targets of violence, techniques used, and nature of movements using violence: e.g., whether government, regime, or community is attacked; whether the attackers are masses or elites; what the goals and ideologies are—nationalistic, reformist, eschatological. Then typologies are constructed based on clusters of variables (Johnson 1964).

One of the most interesting works for the study of modernization is Hobsbawm's *Social Bandits and Primitive Rebels*. Hobsbawm shows that the coming of modern economy disrupts social balances within kinship societies, turning some families into "rich" and others into "poor." Elements of class struggle enter into traditional systems of blood vengeance and outlawry, producing multiplicity of murderous feuds and embittered outlaws. Hobsbawm understands social banditry as endemic peasant protest against oppression and poverty, of righting individual wrongs, stemming from an ambition for a traditional world in which men are justly dealt with, not a new and perfect world (p. 5). Epidemic violence, rather than endemic violence, results when peasant society is in a condition of abnormal tension and disruption. Hobsbawm asserts that social banditry has next to no organization or ideology and is totally inadaptable to modern social

movements. Its most highly developed forms, which skirt
national guerrilla warfare, are rare and themselves ineffective.
The nineteenth and twentieth centuries emerge as the classical ages of social banditry because of disruption of peasant
societies. But after analyzing such movements, Hobsbawm
asserts that they are incapable of helping peasant society because they do not understand social processes. Hobsbawm
also looks at fundamentally reformist groups which remain,
in his words, "prepolitical." These survive, but not as social
movements. They are embryo national movements which
include defense of traditional society and aspirations of
classes and individuals.

Hobsbawm has a set of classifications, and his analysis
shows which movements are more easily modernized than
others. By looking at the structure of movements, their be-
lief systems, their composition, Hobsbawm is able to give us
propositions about which movements can be successfully
integrated into revolutionary movements. He does this both
for rural and urban groups. And he is concerned with direct
use of violence to achieve economic and political changes,
as in riots and rebellions of urban mobs who nonetheless
were in symbiotic relationships with rulers or who had short-
term goals. Hobsbawm sees mobs as empiricist and argues
that the historical failure of Kings and Church led them to
change sides and provided a pool of ready rioters for the
new revolutionaries of the nineteenth century. Thus Hobsbawm's violent men are acting within a changing social context, and he sees violent actions within varying historical
frameworks. His is a detailed study both of the changing
forms and contents of violent movements related to society-
wide change.

AlRoy, too, looks at peasant involvement in internal war and argues that, historically, large-scale insurrection is epidemic in the rural areas where brigandage is endemic. "Where there is Robin Hood, Wat Tyler is not far away." AlRoy stresses that when a peasant insurgency is revolutionary it is transcending its typical character and its leadership is changing in social composition. Why peasants get involved in internal wars, AlRoy says, is not so easy to see. The argument that peasants revolt when they are poor and things are getting worse has been examined critically by De Tocqueville, Brinton, Tilly, Tanter. Mitchell has also denied this in a study on South Vietnam. Russet correlates violence with poverty and dispossessed farmers. Davis also stresses short-term decline in economic growth. The view of the American government seems to be that security means development (see McNamara, *New York Times,* May 19, 1966, for one of many such statements), even if there has been wide recognition that the process of development may feed the flames of insurrection.

Gurr makes the useful suggestion that economic growth rates may not be good indicators of the impact of economic fluctuations on peoples in developing countries. This is particularly true where subsistence sectors still account for large shares of Gross Domestic Product and varying climate conditions may be more important to standards of living than changes in price for exports, which can account for rather mercurial changes in growth rates without anything happening to the structure of the economy.

Those who have concerned themselves primarily with the frequency of domestic violence have tried to account for patterns of frequency and duration. For Huntington (1962),

frequency of violence reflects the prevalence of rapid social
and political change. The causes of insurrectionary violence
are found in the sweeping changes labeled development,
growth, modernization, Westernization, transition, and independence. Huntington interestingly sees a dialectical process between radical and conservative reform coups. The
conservative coups are seldom able to undo change. Modernization emerges not as the product of any one particular
group, however modernized that group may be in compari-
son with the rest of society. Rather it is the product of coup
and countercoup, in which military elements play important
roles in inaugurating both radical and conservative regimes
(p. 36). For a very different view of patterns of coups, see
Springer in Bienen, where the military is seen as exacerbating
regional and social gaps instead of bridging them and where
the military does not build political institutions or itself constitute an effective political organization.

Huntington accounts for lack of violence in developed
countries in terms of mass apathy, end of ideology, and absence of issues. A major question emerges: Can the new violence in developed countries—Canada, America, Belgium,
and Hungary—be accounted for by arguing that subcom-
munities within the developed society are still in transition?
If, as Pye suggests in *Guerrilla Communism in Malaya* (1956),
alienation often has its roots in the rationalism of modern
government, may we not expect violence feeding on alienation in developed societies both because there are many
"nonrational" components within such societies and because alienation in a general way is said to characterize
many modern groups in developed societies? Pye's proposition, that "within highly complex industrial societies, it

is almost impossible for political controversies to develop to the point of sustained and organized violence," is belied by too much of recent American history, not to say French history (Pye 1964, p. 162).

Some of the attempts to get at patterns of violence primarily in developing areas or patterns culled from study of the great revolutions may be useful for approaching violence in economically developed societies. Davis' theory, where it is stated that a moment of potential revolution is reached when long-term growth is followed by short-term declines, would apply in wealthy countries, particularly if his "J" curve applied to other than purely economic satisfaction (see Stone 1966, p. 172).

Theory which looks for the genesis of civil violence in terms of frustration and aggression is suggestive for study of violence in developed countries if only because of emphasis on perception of conditions rather than sole concern with economic growth figures or social mobilization data. The central premise of Gurr's theory is that the necessary precondition for violent civil conflict is relative deprivation, defined as the actors' perception of discrepancy between their value expectations and their environment's value capabilities (p. 3). (I leave aside here questions about whether or not the relative deprivation is treated as a residual category.) The importance of the efforts of Gurr and others lies in the attempt to look at the relevant properties of individual behavior among collectivities (Eckstein's call for the behavioral approach heeded), and to relate these properties to aspects of social structure and processes. Gurr (p. 1) sees the work of Smelser, Zolberg (1966a), Johnson (1964), and Parsons as implicitly or explicitly regarding civil strife as a calculated response to objective social conditions that pays little or no attention to motivational considerations that might explain men's differential responses to the stipulated conditions. However, the merit of Gurr's work at the present time may be in the data collection and processing to find instigating and mediating behaviors in order to get at violent outcomes rather than to be persuasive about the place of motives in the genesis of violence.

Gurr also explains violence in variously defined types of systems. This has the advantage of sensitizing us to explanations for violence which depend on differential characteristics of systems. Mosca, of course, pointed the way to this kind of analysis when he noted that upheavals in small states where a bureaucratic organization does not exist, or exists only in embryonic form, bear only a superficial resemblance to upheavals in large states (p. 199). Mosca also noted that in small states innovations might last only as long as the influence or the life of the author lasted, in terms of establishing less violent and sanguinary regimes. We can again refer to Aristotle for an emphasis on classifying polities in order to understand revolution and violence.

Gurr finds that the strongest core of stability in Latin America is the existence of relatively institutionalized party systems (see Huntington 1966). But one wonders about this when students of Colombia point out that it has been the very existence of institutionalized parties which accounts for the persistence and pervasiveness of violence in that country (Young, Anderson, and Von der Mehden). It is necessary to subject Gurr's and the Feierabends' macroanalyses to this kind of specific query (although not here), which only calls attention to the importance of these efforts.

Before breaking off these remarks on violence and change
and violence and no change, it ought to be said that studies
of revolutions which did not take place as well as studies
which focus on the use of violence in maintaining stability
are crucial in looking at the problem of violent transformation. As has been pointed out, much of contemporary social
science has looked at social stability. Feldman and Eckstein
among others have complained about the lack of treatment
of large-scale violence. Yet implicit in the literature on mechanisms for social cohesion and stability is a concern for
social control. Parsons has recently made this concern quite
explicit. We shall momentarily turn attention to a literature
where use of violence as a form of social control has also
been tied to an analysis of system change—the literature on
totalitarianism. Work on theory of democracy and on democratic systems has taken up the question: Why no violence in
a particular system or under certain circumstances? I have
not referred to this literature at all, but it has a rather ancient pedigree going back to Plato and Aristotle and is highly relevant for approaching the problem of modernization
and violence. Marx, too, can be considered in this tradition
as well as in the corpus of work on violent politics. His concept of false consciousness is directly relevant. Studies of
criminality should throw light on these questions since we
want to know whether, as nonpolitical violence declines
in saliency, political violence rises, and, if so, in what kinds
of society. There are a number of contemporary situations
which raise very interesting questions about why violence
arises in, for example, cities in the Congo prior to 1960,
but not afterward, and not in cities in Colombia during *La
Violencia.* In generally violent and volatile situations, ex-

amination of barriers to violence should tell us a great deal about violence and change.

4. TOTALITARIANISM

The glorification of violence has been seen as a striking feature of totalitarianism (Friedrich; Friedrich and Brzezinski). Two particular functions of violence have been described in the literature on totalitarianism. Prior to the totalitarian movement's assuming power, violence is perceived to be necessary because the movement calls for total destruction of the old society. Since there will be opponents who will resist, they must be treated violently. After the revolutionary power is established, violence continues to be used to impose control over enemies, but the enemy is widely decreed as society itself. Thus, totalitarianism emerges in a number of writings as a system of revolution which seeks to destroy the existing political order by violent means and then to reconstitute a new order, a new man, a new history, also by violence (Friedrich and Brzezinski, p. 131). Terror snowballs because the determination to achieve total change meets the resistance not only of target groups but also of overlapping and interlocking units. The more consensus that is created in society, the more violence can be decentralized or take the form of community pressure and local vengeance (Friedrich). But it has been asserted that totalitarian terror is the vital nerve of the totalitarian system (Friedrich and Brzezinski, p. 132) and that the terror increases in scope and violence as the totalitarian system becomes more stable and firm (p. 137).

Terror here is not seen as simply a device to keep the regime from being overthrown by opponents. Arendt (1958), too, has stressed the function of terror in atomizing society and perpetuating a special kind of rule, rather than merely keeping the government in power. Terror increases as opposition decreases (p. 393). In Friedrich and Brzezinski this is put as follows: Totalitarian terror maintains in institutionalized form the civil war that originally produced the totalitarian movement and by means of which the regime is able to proceed with its program of social disintegration and then social reconstruction (p. 150). The purge is understood as an expression of resiliency and energy of the totalitarian movement and not as an indication of its corruption—and forthcoming disintegration. Purges occur during periods of relative stability, when the leadership can afford them. In Brzezinski's work, the purge is seen as being permanent and preventing stabilization of political forces which might limit the power of the totalitarian leadership. Thus we have the image put forward of a society in constant flux because destabilization is consciously carried out by violence. The totalitarian society fulfills certain criteria for being modern according to the lights of those who see modernization as persistent transformation, although the kinds of societies in view are different and the role of violence is not of equal saliency in both visions. For many observers totalitarian societies are said to be modern technologically and more generally in the economic sphere. But they are often accused of not being "truly" modern because they cannot handle demands for participation. This ignores the fact that totalitarian regimes do handle the problem of participation, albeit in a repressive way and sometimes with recourse to violence.

The relationship of violence and information has been re-marked on. The use of coercion has been seen by Apter as reducing information (Apter 1963, p. 386). For analytical purposes, Apter posits an inverse relationship between in-formation and coercion in a system. Brzezinski sees the ab-solute power of the totalitarian regime isolating it; isolation breeds insecurity; insecurity breeds suspicion and fear; sus-picion and fear breed violence (p. 17). By positing this kind of relationship, one must see some most efficient point be-tween coercion and information (as Apter does); thus there should be self-imposed limits on violence in this system. The totalitarian system or the mobilizing system (Apter uses the latter term) should turn into a modernizing autocracy (another term Apter uses), because no regime wants to either modernize, innovate, or terrorize itself out of existence. Theorists of totalitarianism might answer variously: (1) The instruments of terror get a vested interest in it (Gliksman; Brzezinski). (2) The leaders are not rational or not above all interested in maintaining power. Rather they are men who have a revulsion against society per se. Bronkowski says, "The love of violence is . . . the ancient and symbolic ges-ture of man against the constraints of society." One con-clusion from this is that violence and society themselves stand in inverse proportions. Another reply to the idea of self-limiting violence is that since the government's infor-mation declines as it uses terror it may not realize a thresh-old has been reached as the terror snowballs (Brzezinski). For Arendt, a calculus of rationality and irrationality is no longer useful in describing totalitarian violence. Mass men are superfluous or see themselves as superfluous, and they are taught this by punishment meted out which is unconnected with crime (Arendt 1958, p. 457).

Barrington Moore (1954) has a rather different view. He sees terror as apparently capricious from the point of view of many citizens, but a rational device from the rulers' standpoint (p. 157). Stability in systems where terror is used rests on the fact that many potential victims know the risks and take them or avoid responsibility. Those who work their way to the top are thick-skinned and able to repress doubts and insecurities. This argument ignores certain target groups who did not apparently take risks but who were the recipients of violence anyway: Jews, Volga Germans, relatives of political officials, persons arbitrarily denounced, etc.

Moore (1954) also argues that atomization and destruction of social ties takes place in the course of urbanization and industrialization and is not a consequence of totalitarian regimes alone. This point has been made by those who stress "new states in transition" and by sociologists who have inquired into the social-economic base of violent politics. Lipset has focused on the marginal man who is isolated or operates in isolated social and occupational groups. Pluralism and cross-culture cleavages are seen as barriers against extremist groups. (Also see Kornhauser 1959 and Shils. For a critique of pluralist theories of democracy, see Rogin.) Mass societies undergoing rapid social change are vulnerable to political movements destructive of democratic institutions (Kornhauser 1959; Selznick). An interesting difference between the literature on new states and that on industrial societies is that many writers concerned with the former argue that violence comes about because individuals confuse public and private by seeing private problems as public issues; in the latter, individuals' focus of attention is said to be on remote events (Kornhauser 1959, p. 43). And in works on developing areas, multiple linkages are often seen as transmission belts through which violence is conveyed or which may themselves exacerbate discontent. Much of the literature on ethnicity in developing areas makes the point that violence can come about when individuals and groups get into new relationships along functional, i.e., economic, lines, and begin to perceive ethnic differences as being inimical for the first time. The creation of a web of multiple affiliations may lead to violence; or conflict, when it comes, may be more violent than before.

The use of violence to bring totalitarian movements to power can be described in the same terms as its use in nontotalitarian revolutions. This is true also for violence used to consolidate a regime in the terror phase of a revolution. But the purported use of violence to constantly innovate does provide something new under the sun. Here physical violence must be clearly distinguished from other forms, and it is physical violence we have been referring to. (Those who define terror in terms of disorienting behavior may blur the distinction.) Community pressure and economic coercion are not the same thing as torture and death. Thus those who now argue that the Soviet Union is still characterized by terror and potential violence used in an unrestrained way are still admitting that real changes have taken place since Stalin's death. If it is true that the Cultural Revolution in China is a movement to enlist the enthusiasm of youth in a new reign of violence, to revive a flagging revolutionary spirit (Friedrich then we are more in the realm of permanent revolution throu use of violence. Is this an example of an attempt to overcome backwardness through reliance on institutional mechanisms of violence? Is it the elimination of backwardness which is primarily at stake, or is violence perhaps a substitute for development? That is, does change through violence, at the level of circulating elites, and provision of gratification, through the use of violence and elimination of certain status groups, substitute for change directed at economic growth or alterations in group commitments, social composition, and belief-systems?

Theories of persistent transformation have implicit within them the idea of transformation toward specifiable ends. These ends may not be stated simply as industrialization or economic growth. Rather they are the institutionalization of patterns which make possible continuous change. But the change is *toward* something; it is not change for its own sake, even if this change is somehow shown to be fundamental. No theorists of modernization that I know have argued for the adoption of the vision of totalitarian society which is ascribed to totalitarians by their lay analysts. Persistent transformation has not meant atomization of society to theorists of modernization.

The image of totalitarian society which was put forward either as descriptive of reality or as a polar type toward which real societies approached has come under attack in recent years as being not accurate (in the first usage) or heuristic (in the second). The Soviet Union, even under Stalin, is being portrayed in revisionist literature as having had stable patterns of power relationships—buffers between rulers and ruled, patronage politics—and new conclusions are being drawn from the well-known facts of regime inefficiency.

In reconsideration of the function of violence, more questions than those concerning the post-Stalin end of the Terror are being raised.

As Gundersheim among others has pointed out, studies of totalitarianism emphasized the structural reliance on terrorism rather than legitimation as a means of social control. Those who have tried to account for the comparatively minimal role of physical violence induced by the secret police in China as compared with other totalitarian regimes, have stressed mechanisms by which the regime is able to legitimize itself, to persuade rather than coerce. One possibility, in the light of theories which postulate violence as a consequence of rapid social change, is that China has not had enough social change to account for large-scale violence. This may seem a paradoxical statement, since China has been characterized often in terms of breakdown of traditional peasant society during the anti-Japanese and civil wars. But compared with violence and social change in the Soviet Union, the stressing of obstacles to social change and the minimization of violence in China might be sensible. This proposition would conflict with the hypothesis that the more backward a society, the more may violence be required to overcome relative backwardness. A possible synthesis would be emphasis on creation of institutions (including ideologies) through which change can take place after the revolutionary seizure of power to overcome backwardness. These institutions can perhaps be more easily built where there has not been enough social change to erode all traditional consensus.

CONCLUSIONS

Perhaps we can briefly review some of our findings and then make a few suggestions about possible approaches. [1]

1) With respect to causes of violence, we have, as Eckstein and others have pointed out, an incredible number of factors listed in the literature explaining revolution and its violence, quite a few of which are mutually contradictory. Recently, attempts to explain violence have moved away from structural approaches and have focused instead on behavioral factors, i.e., on the individual and personality factors, or *who* is engaging in violence and *why*. This is an understandable shift in view of the dissatisfaction with past explanations based on social conditions, which can cut so many ways. These new attempts try to measure anger, frustration, and aggression and are characterized by reliance on quantification and factor analysis. Although useful, this approach returns us to where we started, for it does not measure anger and frustration directly but deduces them from social

---

1. I have relied for my summary points on M. Stephen Kaplan's excellent synopsis of my remarks to the Adlai Stevenson Institute of International Affairs, Study Group on Violent Politics, October 28, 1967. This synopsis was included in *Summary of First Session of the Study Group on Violent Politics.*

conditions (e.g., frustration as a ratio of social-want formation to social-want satisfaction). It is quite difficult to find ways to measure anger and frustration—survey research is a questionable tool—but if in fact we deduce behavioral phenomena from social conditions we should at least be clear that we have not measured them directly.

2) In most of the literature on revolution, revolution has been defined in terms of violence, but this simply amounts to explanation by definition. We have a similar problem with thec rists who define "true" revolution as acceptance of violence as the means to change when "all else has failed," which is either a tautological statement or false, depending on the use of "tru

3) In the literature on insurgency, we have competing theor regarding the place of violence. One set of theories sees violenc per se as functional for modernization, as a purging force that makes men modern and makes them whole, thereby preparing them for life in a modernizing society (Fanon, Debray, Mao, Lenin). Another, which represents a response by American the rists, e.g., Rostow, considers espousal of violence as an end in i self to be a fundamentally irrational response to the challenges of modernization by a generation of romantic revolutionaries that is passing from the scene. This irrational response is correlated, in this view, with frustrating conditions which have sty mied development and is the cry of leaders who have been unable to cope with them. Thus, it can be explained as the violence of the "transitional" period. But the American literature on counterinsurgency is peculiar in one respect: those who talk about the "transition" also talk about masses apathetic to some degree, as when they espouse a "high military strategy" of withdrawing or making costly "inputs" needed by guerrillas who they assume are operating in a context of mass

apathy. Yet these same people talk about a "transition" that is defined by an increase in political participation by the masses. Thus, we see the paradox of holding to a view that sees increasing participation by the masses while simultaneously believing that insurgents can be dealt with on their own terms, abstracted from social conditions. This literature also contains the notion that perhaps we should slow up social mobilization, since it may be "dysfunctional" for a society. This view leads to a turning away from a concern for social reform, at least in the short run, on the ground that reform may exacerbate conditions or "disequilibrate" political systems, thereby leading to violence.

There is another part of literature on the use of violence by elites—typified by the work of Mosca and Machiavelli—which is more concerned with social reform and system transformation than are current theorists of counterinsurgency. These theorists are worth exploring further, since they are concerned with those judicious uses of violence by governmental elites which permit them to change societies while staying in the saddle.

4) The literature on ghetto violence is plagued by many of the same problems that are found in the writings on revolution and counterinsurgency. First, like the literature on revolution, it contains vast numbers of causal factors. Second, like the literature on counterinsurgency, it speaks of violence in industrial society as anachronistic, as the acts of people in "transition" from an underdeveloped to a developed state, and hence suggests that it can be treated as we treat insurgency in the new nations. This application of conventional wisdom to the problems of the ghetto is not likely to get us any further than it did when applied to insurgency in developing areas.

5) In the literature on totalitarianism can be found the

most explicit concern for relating violence to constant innovation, or modernization as system-transformation. Terror is seen as being used in a conscious way by leaders for system-transformation, leading to the use of such concepts as "permanent revolution" and "permanent purge" (Arendt, Brzezinski, Friedrich). Two problems stand out in this literature: (1) Although the correspondence of the model of totalitarian society to real societies is never perfect, and as a polar type was never intended to be so, people have tended to forget this. Recent studies of the Soviet Union indicate how much the model must be qualified when speaking of real societies. (2) The literature seems to lead us to a paradox. Totalitarian regimes are seen as societies which constantly innovate through use of terror, while achieving stability through use of repression.

6) The literature also contains works which see violence as an instrument to eliminate backwardness, with the implication that the more backward a society is, the more necessary is the use of violence. It contains, as well, writings which see violence as a substitute for real change or economic growth in which the "outs" simply wish to replace the "ins" without having any alternative conception of authority.

7) Policymakers want to know: Transform what? They are interested in talking, not about transforming systems, but about societies. They are interested in knowing what concrete structures in society should be transformed and how to avoid violence; whereas those who are interested in change through violence want to know how to use specific institutions, what kind of violence, how much violence you need to get what you want, and how you innovate through the use of violence without falling apart. For all the work done

on revolutions, totalitarianism, insurgency, and counterinsurgency, there is no body of knowledge that one would con-
fidently recommend to American policymakers who now
confront violence in America and abroad. We would be hard
put to tell them whether or not they are in an internal-war
situation at home. We would be as hard put to recommend
strategies, or even tactics, to deal with the violence they confront, and which confronts them. Is this because we have not
progressed far enough in studies of violence or in understanding change? The obvious answer is both, since the phenomena
are inextricable in theory and practice. What we want to
know, of course, is the place of violence as a causal factor,
i.e., the kinds of changes that are brought about by violence
and the effects of violence on subsequent political systems.
While a lot of attention has been paid to the place of violence in bringing about change, very little work has been
done on the consequences of outbreaks of violence for subsequent political and economic change. The causes and consequences of violence can be understood only in terms of
kinds of change as distinguishing criteria. It is true that
violence is a heterogeneous phenomenon, one that subsumes many different actions. However, typologies of
kinds of actions, scale, or intensity of violence cannot
get us very far by themselves. The sniper who acts out
his individual desires commits the same kind of action
as the sniper who assassinates on orders of a movement,
but the political act is different in cause and probably in
consequence. We look not for a single theory of violence
but rather for theories of violence and change. A key problem in formulating such theories, which I have only touched
on, is arriving at criteria for change: lacking these we find

no meaningful linkage between violence and change.

Although violence and change must be linked, they must not be treated conceptually as contingent concepts. Most social and political change, including some of the most fundamental change, does not result from violent revolution. Large-scale violence may change nothing; violence often represents a watershed in a slower, more prolonged, and deeper process of transformation, although such watersheds need not be violent. Thus, we ought to avoid definitions of change which build in violence, as many definitions of revolution do. Criteria of change can be specified without reference to whethe or not violence takes place. Then violence can be measured for intensity, scope, and duration (and one of the advantages we have in the study of violent politics is that such measurements can be made). But the measurements have meaning only when they are placed in the context of various kinds and degrees of change. Then it is possible to try and find correlations between violence and change.

Despite my pessimistic conclusions about how much light we have been able to shed on critical problems, we do not start from scratch in the study of violent politics and modernization. There is an accumulation of data both from case studies and from cross-national surveys which can be used in the forming and testing of propositions. There is also data from comparative historical studies which has not been mined specifically for the study of violence and change. Similarly, there has been work done on motivation which does try to measure directly for psychological variables which are not reducible to social structural theory. Work done in psychology has barely been tapped for insights into violent politics. Moreover, some approaches do not see violence as an extraordinary event but rather something which can be used by elites, counterelites, and nonelites both for perpetuation of rule and social transformation. There are also those who have argued that violence may become institutionalized, may become part of the very functioning of a system. (Machiavelli and Mosca among others approach violent politics this way.)

It would be nice to end on a positive note and say that we can expect new theories which will integrate analyses of violence and change and which will reveal to us the connections between them. But can we? Indeed, theoretical frameworks for the study of violence and modernization have been found wanting. Our hope is to formulate a theory, in the sense of deductive theory, which explains and predicts empirical facts relating to violence and change from a few axioms. Theory, in this sense, is a set of propositions derived from the axioms and from which predictions are made, as Homans, among others, has pointed out. Perhaps more empirical work on individual motivation and on total societies will allow us to make the kinds of theoretical assumptions (axioms) necessary for this kind of theory. Most theorizing in the social sciences has not, in any case, been theory in the sense just used above and which prevails in the physical sciences. Rather it has meant postulating concepts and definitions, and often simply retranslating from one language of definition to another without hypothesizing anything.

I remain agnostic about the possibilities for constructing theories of violence and change in the deductive manner. But I am convinced of the need for improving on analysis of violence and change by creating conceptual frameworks in which violence and modernization are not thought of as separate categories and separate areas of study to begin with. Definitions always have a degree of arbitrariness to them. I said earlier that adjectives which modify change, such as "rapid" and "transforming," created difficulties for me precisely because when we think of a changed social system or a social system which is maintained we must state arbitrarily what we mean by "change" or "same." Nonetheless, it may be useful to do this. For once we specify what we mean by change, we may then begin to look at the place of violence in the changes we specify. The definitions of violence and change, I said, ought not to be contingent one on the other. However, we should be aware that definitions have varying appropriateness in different contexts. Thus a definition of change which will be useful in thinking about a caterpillar turning into a butterfly may not be very useful for thinking about violent politics. And thinking about violence on the football field ought to involve different concepts than thinking about violent politics. As William Kornhauser has put it, "The readiness to assimilate all politics to either order or violence implies a very narrow notion of order and a very broad notion of violence . . . what is violent action in one period of history becomes acceptable conflict at a later time" (Kornhauser 1968). It is with this in mind that I have said violence and modernization must be linked so that we can refine our concepts for the context with which we are concerned.

BIBLIOGRAPHY

Almond, Gabriel A., and Coleman, James S., eds. 1960.
   The Politics of the Developing Areas. Princeton, N.J.:
   Princeton University Press.

AlRoy, Gil C. 1966. *The Involvement of Peasants in Internal
   Wars.* Center of International Studies, Princeton University,
   Research Monograph No. 24, Princeton, N.J.

Apter, David. 1963. "Political Religion in the New Nations."
   In Clifford Geertz, ed., *Old Societies and New States.*
   Glencoe, Ill.: Free Press.

———. 1965. *The Politics of Modernization.* Chicago:
   University of Chicago Press.

Arendt, Hannah. 1958. *The Origins of Totalitarianism.*
   New York: Meridian Books.

———. 1963. *On Revolution.* New York: Viking Press.

Bendix, Reinhard. 1964. *Nation-Building and Citizenship.*
   New York: Wiley & Sons.

Bienen, Henry, ed. 1968. *The Military Intervenes: Case
   Studies in Political Development.* New York: Russell Sage.

Blauner, Robert. 1966. "Whitewash over Watts." *Trans-
   action,* vol. 3, no. 3 (March-April).

Brinton, Crane. 1962. *Anatomy of Revolution.* New York:
   Prentice-Hall.

Brzezinski, Zbigniew. 1956. *The Permanent Purge.*
   Cambridge: Harvard University Press.

Carmichael, Stokely, and Hamilton, Charles. 1967. *Black Power.* New York: Random House.

Carr, E. H. 1964. *Studies in Revolution.* New York: Grosset & Dunlap.

Coser, Lewis. 1956. *The Functions of Social Conflict.* Glencoe, Ill.: Free Press.

———. 1966. "Internal Violence as a Mechanism for Conflict Resolution." Paper presented to the Working Group on Armed Forces and Society, International Sociological Association, Evian.

Cruse, Harold. 1967. *The Crisis of the Negro Intellectual.* New York: Morrow.

Dahrendorf, R. 1959. *Class and Class Conflict in Industrial Society.* Stanford, Calif.: Stanford University Press.

Davis, James C. 1962. "Towards a Theory of Revolution." *American Sociological Review* 27 (February): 1-19.

Debray, Regis. 1967. "Revolution in the Revolution?" *Monthly Review,* vol. 19 (July-August).

Dudley, Bill. 1965. "Violence in Nigerian Politics." *Transition* 5, no. 21: 21-24.

Eckstein, Harry. 1963. "Internal War: The Problem of Anticipation." In Ithiel de Sola *et al., Social Science Research and National Security.* Washington, D.C.: Smithsonian Institution.

Eckstein, Harry, ed. 1964. *Internal War.* New York: Macmillan Co.

Engels, Friedrich. 1947. *Herr Eugen Dühring's Revolution in Science* (Anti-Dühring). Moscow: Foreign Languages Publishing House.

Fanon, Frantz. 1966. *The Wretched of the Earth.* New York: Grove Press.

Feierabend, Ivo K., and Feierabend, Rosalind L. 1966. "Aggressive Behaviors within Polities, 1948-1962: A Cross National Study." *Journal of Conflict Resolution* 10, no. 3 (September): 240-71.

Feldman, Arnold. 1964. "Violence and Volatility." In Harry Eckstein, ed., *Internal War*. New York: Macmillan Co.

Friedrich, Carl. 1967. "The Changing Theory and Practice of Totalitarianism." Paper presented to the American Political Science Association Meeting, Chicago, September.

Friedrich, Carl, and Brzezinski, Z. 1961. *Totalitarian Dictatorship and Autocracy*. New York: Frederick A. Praeger.

Geertz, Clifford. 1963. "Primordial Sentiments and Civil Politics in the New States." In *Old Societies and New States*, edited by Clifford Geertz. Glencoe, Ill.: Free Press.

———. 1968. "We Can Claim No Special Gift for Violence." In "Is America by Nature a Violent Society?" *New York Times Magazine*, April 28, p. 25.

Gerschenkron, Alexander. 1962. *Economic Backwardness in Historical Perspective*. Cambridge: Harvard University Press.

———. 1964. "Reflections on the Economic Aspects of Revolution." In Harry Eckstein, ed., *Internal War*. New York: Macmillan Co.

Giap, Vo Nguyen. 1962. *People's War, People's Army*. New York: Frederick A. Praeger.

Glazer, Nathan, and Moynihan, Daniel. 1963. *Beyond the Melting Pot*. Cambridge, Mass.: M.I.T. Press.

Gliksman, Jerzy. 1963. "Social Prophylaxis as a Form of Terror." In Carl Friedrich, ed., *Totalitarianism*. New York: Grosset & Dunlap.

Greene, T. N., ed. 1962. *The Guerrilla and How To Fight Him*. New York: Frederick A. Praeger.

Grimshaw, Allen. 1962. "Factors Contributing to Colour Violence in the United States and Britain." *Race,* vol. 3 (May).

———. 1963*a*. "Three Major Cases of Colour Violence in the United States." *Race* 5 (July): 76-86.

———. 1963*b*. "Actions of Police and Military in American Race Riots." *Phylon*, Fall.

———. 1963*c*. "Police Agencies and the Prevention of Racial Violence." *Journal of Criminal Law, Criminology, and Police Science* 54 (March): 110-13.

Guevara, Ché. 1961. *On Guerrilla Warfare.* Edited by H. C. Peterson. New York: Frederick A. Praeger.

Gundersheim, Arthur. 1966. "Terror and Political Control in Communist China." Unpublished paper.

Gurr, Ted, with Ruttenberg, Charles. 1967. *The Conditions of Civil Violence: First Tests of a Causal Model.* Center of International Studies, Princeton University, Research Monograph No. 28. Princeton, N.J.

Haimson, Leopold. 1955. *The Russian Marxists and the Origins of Bolshevism.* Cambridge: Harvard University Press.

Halpern, Manfred. 1964. "Toward Further Modernization of the Study of New Nations." *World Politics* 17, no. 3 (October): 157-81.

Harrington, James. 1924. *The Commonwealth of Oceana (1656).* Arendt cites two editions, Indianapolis, Ind.: Liberal Arts; Heidelberg: Liljegren.

Hayden, Tom. 1967. "Occupation of Newark." *New York Review of Books,* August 25.

Hilsman, Roger. 1962. "Internal War: The New Communist Tactic." In T. N. Greene, ed., *The Guerrilla and How To Fight Him.* New York: Frederick A. Praeger.

Hobsbawm, Eric. 1959. *Social Bandits and Primitive Rebels.* Glencoe, Ill.: Free Press.

Hodgkin, Thomas. 1964. "The Relevance of Western Ideas for the New African States." In J. Roland Pennock, ed., *Self-Government in Modernizing Nations.* Englewood Cliffs, N.J.: Prentice-Hall.

Homans, George C. 1964. "Contemporary Theory in Sociology." In R. Faris, ed., *Handbook of Modern Sociology.* Chicago: Rand McNally.

Howard, Anthony. 1967. "Detroit's Travail: Why?" *Courier-Journal* (Louisville), August 3.

Huntington, Samuel P. 1962. "Patterns of Violence in World Politics." In S. P. Huntington, ed., *Changing Patterns of Military Politics.* Glencoe, Ill.: Free Press.

———. 1966. "Political Development and Political Decay." *World Politics,* vol. 17 (April).

Janowitz, Morris. 1968. *Social Control of Escalated Riots.* Chicago: University of Chicago Center for Policy Study.

Johnson, Chalmers. 1962a. *Peasant Nationalism and Communist Power: The Emergence of Revolutionary Power.* Stanford, Calif.: Stanford University Press.

———. 1962b. "Civilian Loyalties and Guerrilla Conflicts." *World Politics,* vol. 14, no. 4 (July).

———. 1964. *Revolution and the Social System.* Hoover Institution Studies 3, Stanford University. Stanford, Calif.

———. 1967. *Revolutionary Change.* Boston: Little, Brown & Co.

Kling, Merle. 1956. "Towards a Theory of Power and Political Instability in Latin America." *Western Political Quarterly,* vol. 9.

Kornhauser, William. 1959. *The Politics of Mass Society.*
Glencoe, Ill.: Free Press.

———. 1964. "Rebellion and Political Development." In
Harry Eckstein, ed., *Internal War.* New York: Macmillan
Co.

———. 1968. "Conflict, Order, and Change at Berkeley."
Unpublished discussion paper.

Kroes, Rob. 1966. "Revolution and Scientific Knowledge."
Paper presented to the Working Group on Armed Forces
and Society, Evian.

Lambert, Richard. 1950. Unpublished paper presented before Seminar on Social Tensions, UNESCO, New Delhi.
Referred to in Grimshaw (1963*b*).

Lasch, Christopher. 1968. "The Trouble with Black Power."
New York Review of Books, February 29, pp. 4-14.

Lenin, V. 1932. *State and Revolution.* New York: International Publishers.

———. 1962. *Partisan Warfare.* In Franklin Mark Osanka, ed.,
Modern Guerrilla Warfare. Glencoe, Ill.: Free Press.

Le Vine, Victor T. 1965. "The Course of Political Violence."
In William H. Lewis, ed., *French Speaking Africa.* New
York: Walker.

Levy, Marion J., Jr. 1964. "A Revision of the *Gemeinschaft-
Gesellschaft* Categories and Some Aspects of the Inter-
dependencies of Minority and Host Systems." In Harry
Eckstein, ed., *Internal War.* New York: Macmillan Co.

———. 1967. " 'Does It Matter if He's Naked?' Bawled the
Child." Unpublished paper.

Leys, Colin. 1965. "Violence in Africa." *Transition* 5,
no. 21: 17-20.

Lieberson, Stanley, and Silverman, Arnold. 1965. "The

Precipitants and Underlying Conditions of Race Riots."
American Sociological Review, 30: 887-98.

Lipset, Seymour Martin. 1963. *Political Man: The Social
Bases of Politics.* New York: Doubleday & Co.

McAlister, John T., Jr. Forthcoming. *Vietnam: The Origins
of Revolution.* New York: Alfred Knopf.

Mao Tse-tung. 1960. *On the Protracted War.* Peking: Foreign
Languages Press.

Moore, Barrington. 1954. *Terror and Progress in the USSR.*
Cambridge: Harvard University Press.

———. 1966. *Social Origins of Dictatorship and Democracy.*
Boston: Beacon Press.

Mosca, Gaetano. 1965. *The Ruling Class.* New York:
McGraw-Hill.

Osanka, Franklin Mark, ed. 1962. *Modern Guerrilla Warfare.*
Glencoe, Ill.: Free Press.

Paret, Peter, and Shy, John W. 1962. *Guerrillas in the 1960's.*
Rev. ed. New York: Frederick A. Praeger.

Pustay, John S. 1965. *Counter-insurgency Warfare.* New York:
Macmillan Co.

Pye, Lucien W. 1956. *Guerrilla Communism in Malaya.*
Princeton, N.J.: Princeton University Press.

———. 1962. *Politics, Personality, and Nation Building:
Burma's Search for Identity.* New Haven, Conn.: Yale
University Press.

———. 1964. "The Roots of Insurgency and Commencement
of Rebellions." In Harry Eckstein, ed., *Internal War.*
New York: Macmillan Co.

*Report of the National Advisory Commission on Civil Dis-
orders.* 1968. New York: Bantam Books.

Rogin, Michael Paul. 1967. *The Intellectuals and McCarthy.*
Cambridge, Mass.: M.I.T. Press.

Rostow, W. W. 1962. "Guerrilla Warfare in Underdeveloped

Areas." In T. N. Greene, ed., *The Guerrilla and How To Fight Him.* New York: Frederick A. Praeger.

Russett, Bruce. 1964. "Inequality and Instability: The Relationship of Land Tenure to Politics." *World Politics* 16: 442-54.

Rustin, Bayard. 1966. "The Watts Manifesto and the McCone Report." *Commentary* 41, no. 3 (March): 29-35.

———. 1967. "A Way out of the Exploding Ghetto." *New York Times Magazine,* August 13.

Sathyamurthy, T. V. 1965. "Revolutions and Revolutionaries." *Transition* 5, no. 21: 25-32.

Schram, Stuart, ed. and trans. 1963. *Political Thought of Mao Tse-tung.* New York: Frederick A. Praeger.

Schurmann, Herbert F. 1966. *Ideology and Organization in Communist China.* Berkeley and Los Angeles: University of California Press.

Shannon, William V. 1967a. "Negro Violence vs. the American Dream." *New York Times,* July 27.

———. 1967b. "Two Faces of the Negro Revolution." *New York Times,* July 30.

Shils, Edward. 1956. *The Torment of Secrecy.* Glencoe, Ill.: Free Press.

Smelser, Neil J. 1963. *Theory of Collective Behavior.* New York: Macmillan Co.

Stone, Lawrence. 1966. "Theories of Revolution." *World Politics* 18 (January): 159-76.

———. 1967. Review of Barrington Moore's *Social Origins of Dictatorship.* In *New York Review of Books,* August 24

Tanter, Raymond. 1966. "Dimensions of Conflict Behavior within and between Nations, 1958-1960." *Journal of Conflict Resolution* 10, no. 1 (March): 41-65.

Tilly, Charles. 1964. *The Vendée.* Cambridge: Harvard
    University Press.
Wolfe, Charles. 1967. *United States Policy and the Third
    World.* Boston: Little, Brown & Co.
Wolin, Sheldon. 1960. *Politics and Vision.* Boston:
    Little, Brown & Co.
Young, Crawford; Anderson, Charles; and Mehden, Fred
    von der. 1967. *Issues of Political Development.*
    Englewood Cliffs, N.J.: Prentice-Hall.
Zolberg, Aristide. 1964. *One-Party Government in the
    Ivory Coast.* Princeton, N.J.: Princeton University Press.
———. 1966*a.* "The Structure of Political Conflict in the New
    States of Tropical Africa." Paper presented for the Amer-
    ican Political Science Association, New York, September.
———. 1966*b.* "A Gospel for the Damned." *Encounter,*
    November, pp. 56-63.

INDEX

118   *Index*